Linked to Someone in Pain

Linked to Someone in Pain

Cheryl L. Sanfacon, M.D.
and Joyce Magnin Moccero

VICTOR BOOKS
A DIVISION OF SCRIPTURE PRESS PUBLICATIONS INC.
USA CANADA ENGLAND

Scripture quotations are from *The Living Bible,* © 1971, Tyndale House Publishers, Wheaton, IL 60189. Used by permission. Other quotations are from the *Holy Bible, New International Version®* (NIV). Copyright © 1973, 1978, 1984 by International Bible Society. Used by permission of Zondervan Publishing House. All rights reserved.

Copyediting: Carole Streeter and Barbara Williams
Cover Design: Scott Rattray

Library of Congress Cataloging-in-Publication Data

Sanfacon, Cheryl L.
Linked to someone in pain / by Cheryl L. Sanfacon and Joyce Magnin Moccero.
p. cm.
ISBN 1-56476-117-7
1. Mentally ill—Family relationships. 2. Psychotherapy patients—Family relationships. 3. Adjustment (Psychology) 4. Mental illness—Religious aspects—Christianity. 5. Mental illness. I. Moccero, Joyce Magnin. II. Title.
RC455.4.F3S25 1993
616.89—dc20 93-20922
CIP

---

1 2 3 4 5 6 7 8 9 10 Printing/Year 97 96 95 94 93

Contents

For Dennis

CLS

For Peter and our beautiful girls
Rebekah and Emily

JMM

To the Reader

Recovery from emotional pain is a journey that will take your wife, husband, or other loved one through many deep and treacherous waters. It is also a journey that will sail over calm seas and even sit for a while in the doldrums.

Watching a spouse or friend wrestle with emotional difficulties can leave you feeling lost and bewildered. Lost, because it is often hard to know which leg of the journey he or she is traveling. Bewildered, because of your own feelings of confusion, guilt, anger, and even depression as you experience the journey more as a spectator than a participant.

This book presents you an opportunity to become involved in your loved one's recovery. It will also help you learn self-care at a time when you may be feeling most alone.

Fortunately, you are not alone. As you read these pages you will see your own feelings, thoughts, and experiences reflected in people who have been through it.

The journey of self-discovery cannot be solitary. You are a vital link, a necessary cog in the wheel that drives the process. This is your book. It is a resource for those who experience recovery on the other side of the therapist's door.

If I can stop one heart from breaking,
I shall not live in vain;
If I can ease one life the aching,
Or cool one pain,
Or help one fainting robin
Unto his nest again,
I shall not live in vain.

Emily Dickinson

PART 1

Chapter One
Facing Facts

"It never occurred to me that I would one day be driving my wife to a . . . a cracker factory," David announced. "Those places are for crazy people, not you! You're my wife! The mother of our children! A Christian . . . or so I thought."

His voice burst with anger as he dropped the gearshift into drive. "How could you be doing this to me? To the kids?" David banged the palm of his hand on the steering wheel. "The kids . . . what do I tell the kids?"

Elizabeth sat rigid and unshaken. David wasn't sure if she had even heard his words. She held her hands in her lap, fingers locked like a child's during a mealtime prayer.

Just forty-five minutes earlier I had telephoned David to

alert him to the seriousness of Elizabeth's condition.

"You must get her to the hospital," I said. "She's very upset. Suicidal."

I could tell from the dead-weight silence on the other end of the phone line that David was feeling as though he had just been hit by a train.

"David," I said, "I can call the police, but I'd prefer she went calmly with you. It would just be better."

"The hospital? Suicidal?" he said finally. "That can't be true. She's not crazy. She is not that depressed."

"I still want you to come into my office. I can't let her leave in her present condition."

By the time David arrived, Elizabeth had settled down and was talking about going home. I still wasn't convinced she had changed her mind.

David sat across from her. He nervously rubbed his hand on the arm of the blue chair. "I don't get it," he said. "She looks fine, not like she belongs in a mental institution."

"I still recommend you take her to the hospital," I said. "I'm concerned she might hurt herself. Sometimes people who are thinking about suicide appear calm and settled. Sometimes it's a clue that they have made a decision."

David swallowed hard. "Why doesn't she just snap out of it?" he blurted. "Her life is not this bad."

"I've already made the necessary arrangements. They'll be expecting you."

Elizabeth didn't move except to straighten her back against the chair and push some stray brown hairs behind her ear.

I went on to explain that what I had arranged wasn't a "302" or involuntary commitment. David and Elizabeth still had a choice. At that moment I sensed David didn't know what was right. He didn't know what Elizabeth needed.

"I thought therapy was supposed to prevent this," he said as he took his wife by the arm. "I don't understand."

I put my hand on Elizabeth's shoulder. "I'll be in touch."

Elizabeth nodded. "Okay," she said. "You'll know where to find me."

The Hospital

A young nurse in green surgical garb met them at the door. David could feel his heart start to pound faster as the nurse unlocked the heavy door. "You'll have to leave your handbag with your husband," she told Elizabeth. "And then I have to search you."

Elizabeth handed the brown purse to David. He winced as the nurse slowly ran her hands down Elizabeth's pant legs. David tried to make sense of Elizabeth's expression. He searched her tired, puffy eyes. *Let's just go home,* he thought. *You don't need this. You're not like those people in there.*

Then the nurse quickly took Elizabeth by the arm and led her through a large, steel doorway.

A quick, cold shiver surprised David when he heard the thick door close and lock. *What are they going to do with her?* The anger he had felt at the doctor's office melted into concern and questions.

David thought he had stepped into another world. Nothing was right, not even the smell. It wasn't as antiseptic as he knew hospitals to be. In this small bowel of the hospital, he was overtaken more with the smell of perspiration and anguish.

The waiting room was cold and impersonal. There were no magazines to read, no television, no soda machines. The plastic orange chairs were bolted to the floor. Even the black and chrome ashtray was chained down.

David had no idea what was going on behind the locked

door. All the nurse would tell him was that the doctor would see Elizabeth soon.

So he waited and waited and wondered. *This is what's crazy,* he thought. *Sitting here and not knowing what's going on.*

After two long hours Elizabeth walked back through the steel doorway. "He's letting me go," she said. "I correctly named the last three presidents and told him I wasn't suicidal anymore. I said I wanted to go home."

"That took two hours?" asked David.

"Oh, we talked about more than presidents and suicide. I guess he just wanted to make sure I wasn't crazy."

David left the hospital with Elizabeth that night, relieved to have her by his side. He also left the hospital with many questions and concerns. Until this incident Elizabeth's therapy was mostly a mystery. It was simply something she did two or three times a week.

If Elizabeth chose to tell him about her sessions it was fine, and he would listen. He rarely understood or questioned what was going on behind the closed door of the therapist's office.

Now, for the first time in over a year, David saw that he needed to become more involved. He saw how much Elizabeth needed him to be a participant in her recovery, not merely a spectator.

The story that follows chronicles the experiences of David, Elizabeth, and their two children. They are a real family. We have changed names and particularities to protect their privacy.

Although we opened this book with a flashback, the story begins when Elizabeth first started having nightmares. It continues through the time of Elizabeth's suicide threat and then her eventual healing and termination of therapy.

As their story unfolds we will point out similarities between them and any family with a loved one in recovery.

We have included concrete ideas about how to be supportive and to exercise self-care.

Paradise Lost

David and Elizabeth had been married fifteen years when Elizabeth started having symptoms. Marriage and family life were good. Together they had two children and had weathered many storms.

Then life started to unravel. At first it was only a few strands coming loose when Elizabeth's nightmares began. Usually she could shake the dream away and get back to sleep. Most of the time she did not disturb David.

Within a month the dreams became more intense and Elizabeth awakened terrified and screaming. She would leap out of bed and demand that David leave the room. He was shocked and he protested, but Elizabeth's fear was so staggering and so different from anything he had experienced before that he left.

For several nights the scene was repeated as Elizabeth woke up screaming. Each night David slept on the couch as his wife cried, alone, in their bedroom. Each night David comforted their children. "Mom will be all right," he said. "It's only a dream."

Eventually Elizabeth could sleep without the recurring nightmare. On the surface her life had returned to normal. Deep down inside, though, she felt troubled. She knew something had gone terribly wrong. Although the nightmare had vanished, she drifted into a deep depression. Elizabeth's world started to cave in around her, and there was nothing she could do to stop the walls from crumbling.

Over the next several months, David and the children watched Elizabeth's appetite nearly disappear. They stood helplessly by as she grew more and more disinterested in life.

David prayed hard that Elizabeth would get better. But she just couldn't shake the centrifugal pull of depression.

Church activities were no longer important. Household chores became huge mountains to move. Often the children would go to school wearing yesterday's socks. Simple tasks, such as grocery shopping or returning videos to the store, became practically impossible.

Elizabeth would have terrifying panic attacks as she approached the store. Intellectually, she knew doom and destruction were not lurking behind every turn of the aisle, but for no clear reason her heart would pound. She had trouble breathing and felt dizzy as though she were about to pass out and die at any moment.

Elizabeth's feelings about herself and her family fell so low that it didn't seem worth the trouble to get out of bed in the morning.

"You can't stay like this," David said. "You have to get out of bed. You have to eat and clean and shop. You have to take care of the kids and me."

Elizabeth didn't want to do anything. There just wasn't any point. But every day she would try. David knew she wanted to please him and care for the children. She cooked meals and kept the house tidy enough to get by. She would listen to David talk about his work. She helped the kids with homework and made them snacks and treats.

Still David knew Elizabeth was feeling pain in a place he couldn't touch. Although she tried to keep up with daily needs, her spirit was crushed.

The Route into Counseling

People come into counseling for a variety of reasons and in a variety of ways. For some it is a psychiatric emergency. For others it is a final effort to solve problems and understand behaviors. Some find themselves forced to seek counseling after a traumatic event, such as rape or other crime, or the death of a loved one.

Elizabeth took a route into therapy that many people take. First, she recognized and admitted to herself that something was wrong. And since emotional struggles quite often set off physical symptoms such as Elizabeth was having, she made an appointment with her family doctor.

Recognizing a Panic Attack

A sudden episode of terror and feeling of impending doom

SYMPTOMS INCLUDE:
chest pains
palpitations
shortness of breath
dizziness
tingling in hands and feet
sweating
nausea
fear of losing control

David and Elizabeth went to see their family physician together. David listened from one corner of the room as Elizabeth told him about her fatigue and headaches and upset stomach. She told him how she felt the world was closing in around her and she was going to suffocate. She told him that she could feel her heart beating and that she felt dizzy in stores and at church.

David had heard the words before. Now it sounded different. Sitting in the doctor's office, he could not just shake it off. *What if she is ill?* he thought. David began to conjure up images of brain tumors and raging cancers as the doctor examined Elizabeth.

"I can't find anything physical," said the doctor. "I'll

run a few blood tests to be certain. But I'm not the doctor for you."

"What do you mean?" asked David, rising to his feet.

The doctor took a deep breath. "She needs a psychiatrist. Her physical symptoms are from emotional causes. She's severely depressed. She's having what we call panic attacks. They can be very frightening and often can mimic heart attacks or suffocation."

Although relieved that Elizabeth was physically healthy, David now had to worry about her mental health. He didn't know how to do that. Although he couldn't tell Elizabeth, he would rather have been dealing with cancer.

Feeling Guilty

David deeply loved Elizabeth and didn't really wish she had cancer. It was just that cancer is much more acceptable. At least it is something he could tell his mother. But could he really tell his family that Elizabeth was mentally ill? No way! David was on his own.

It didn't take long for another ugly monster that desires to devour our self-esteem to show up—*guilt.*

For David, as for many spouses and loved ones, guilt showed up with a double-barreled shotgun. One side was loaded with feelings of inadequacy. The other was loaded with anger.

Guilt feelings often arise when someone we love is suffering. Love tells us to make it all better, to take the pain away. When we can't, we feel guilty.

Because David saw his wife's needs to be greater than his own, he convinced himself that he didn't have needs anymore, since he was certain Elizabeth couldn't meet them. He was going to be the perfect, understanding husband. After all, Elizabeth didn't have room for him and his needs.

When anyone, no matter how emotionally strong, is not

getting their needs met, they will eventually suffer burnout and feelings of neglect and emptiness. That is usually when the second shot is fired and the spouse winds up angry and feeling even more guilty because he's angry.

What David experienced is normal. It's human and okay. What is not helpful is for anyone to stuff those feelings away like so much dirty laundry.

Sometimes we stuff feelings as a way of helping and protecting our friend or loved one. It might work for a little while, but eventually feelings find their way to the surface, usually in ways we feel sorry about later.

We need to find someone to talk to about it before the hamper gets overloaded and spills on everyone.

Chapter Two
Code Crazy

"You've been awfully quiet," Elizabeth said as David pulled the car into the garage. "Are you upset with what the doctor said?"

David turned the ignition off and took the key from the column. "I'm not sure," he answered. "Let's just go in the house."

Elizabeth filled the tea kettle with water and placed it on the stove. "It's getting chilly out," she said, rubbing her arms. "How about a cup of tea?"

"No thanks," said David. "How can you think about tea now? For a month I've been after you to eat and drink. Nothing happened. And now, after one short visit with the doctor, you want tea."

Just then, three-year-old Anna came running into the kitchen. "Mama," she cried, "Daniel hit me and turned off my movie."

"I did not," hollered nine-year-old Daniel from the family room. "She's such a liar."

Elizabeth gave Anna a hug and patted her on the back. "Just go find a toy to play with, and I'll read you a story in a little while."

David shook his head. "I don't get it," he said. "If this had happened yesterday, you would have started crying. What gives?"

Elizabeth poured boiling water into a mug. "Maybe it just feels good to have someone listen to me finally."

"Oh, no." said David. "Don't bait me."

Anna tugged at Elizabeth's sleeve. "Are you guys gonna fight again?"

"No," answered Elizabeth. "Now run along."

"I'm not so sure," said David. "I think you *want* to see this shrink. Why can't you just talk to me or someone at church?"

Elizabeth sat at the kitchen table. "Because I think Dr. Vernon is right. I need help. More than you or anyone at church can give me right now." Elizabeth combed her fingers through her hair. "I can't believe I just said that."

"I can't believe it either," said David. "You're really going through with this? You're going to let someone label you. She'll say you're crazy. What about your reputation? What if someone finds out? What about the kids?"

"Elizabeth poured the rest of her tea down the drain. "My reputation?" she questioned. "What about my happiness?" She started to cry. "I'm just so tired. I can't live like this. Every day is harder than the one before. I have to convince myself that it's safe to go into the market, for heaven's sake. I need help."

David was quiet a moment. "Go ahead." he said. "Make

the appointment. But leave me out of it. I know you're not crazy."

What Is Crazy?

David was right. Elizabeth wasn't crazy.

Crazy is a word that has come to describe many things we don't understand—including emotional or mental illness. It has become a handy tag to pin on someone who is struggling with deep emotional issues. It has also become a bad word, a word no one would choose to pin on themselves, or on someone they care about deeply.

The truth is that very few people who seek professional counseling are crazy, or have lost touch with reality, or will in the future. Someone does not have to act like Norman Bates in the movie *Psycho* to see a counselor. Yet, sadly, that is the image society has decided fits someone in emotional distress. The word *crazy* has become a term too closely associated with anyone in counseling for any type of problem, from depression to paranoid schizophrenia. It has extremely negative connotations.

According to a *Time* magazine article entitled, "It Hurts Like Crazy!" headline writers and Hollywood producers have helped reinforce an inaccurate link between mental illness and violence.[1]

Actually, a very small percentage of the mentally ill are considered dangerous. Most mentally ill patients are withdrawn, frightened, and passive.

I vividly remember a time when I was an intern, working in an emergency room, a woman came in who was hallucinating. She was hearing voices and was very delusional. I heard the nurse call out, "There's a Code Crazy here." My heart went out to that woman. How demeaning for anyone to be called a Code Crazy. This woman had a different kind of pain, the kind you couldn't cure with sutures and Band-Aids.

What Is Mental Health?

The definition of good mental health can be broken into two simple components. The first is the ability to work and play with satisfaction and fulfillment. The second is the ability to love God, self, and others, also with satisfaction and fulfillment.

This model of mental health is seen throughout Scripture, beginning with the Genesis account of Creation. On the sixth day God made man and immediately gave him dominion over the earth. Adam had the responsibility to work the land and care for the animals.

Likewise, woman was created and given to Adam as a helper in the Garden of Eden. This is where we see the first part of our definition of good mental health—the ability to work with satisfaction and fulfillment.

The second part of the model is summarized in Jesus' words to the Pharisees. He said, " 'Love the Lord your God with all your heart, soul and mind.' This is the first and greatest commandment. The second most important is similar: 'Love your neighbor as much as you love yourself' " (Matthew 22:37-39).

Man and woman were originally created to be physically, emotionally, and spiritually perfect. But because of disobedience in the Garden of Eden, mental illness—beginning with emotional pain, fear, and shame—was introduced into the world, along with physical deterioration, and spiritual and moral separation from God.

Mental Illness Is Nothing New

In the fifth century A.D., the great Greco-Roman physician Caelius Aurelianus wrote that the signs of approaching melancholy (depression) were "anguish and distress, dejections, silence, animosity . . . sometimes a longing for death, suspicion on the part of the patient that a plot is being hatched against him."[2]

In the Psalms, King David spoke many times of his depression. There were times when he cried out to the Lord, pleading that his anguish would end. At other times, he was unable to sleep, and even his bones were afflicted.

Although King David's emotional problems were limited to deep depression, he knew about other types of emotional illness. According to 1 Samuel 21, David feigned insanity as a way to save his life.

Even Jesus fell into the snare of depression. He was a Man of Sorrows acquainted with grief. It was in the Garden of Gethsemane that we hear Jesus say, "My soul is crushed with horror and sadness to the point of death.... Stay here... stay awake with me" (Matthew 26:38). But who would call Jesus Christ or King David crazy? Instead, we feel compassion and empathy for them. Perhaps we even find permission within their words to allow ourselves to feel the pain of depression, anxiety, or mental stress. Instead of being called "code crazy," perhaps those people who are willing to admit and accept their emotional struggles should be called courageous.

Pain Has a Purpose

Physical pain is the body's way of signaling that something is broken or bleeding, or even that cancer cells have invaded the bloodstream. In the same way emotional pain points to sometimes old and festering wounds inside our mind and heart and soul that need attention, care, and healing.

Unfortunately, when it comes to issues of the mind or the body or even the spirit, it is human nature to deny and ignore the symptoms.

So often we hear stories of people who waited too long to see a doctor about a "little lump" or "occasional pain"; when they finally go, it is too late and they live with crippling disease or die.

It usually isn't until people are so depressed that they have stopped eating or working, or are so filled with anxiety that the outdoors has become too scary to venture into, that they seek help.

In his book *The Masks of Melancholy,* John White writes:

> God still heals miraculously. But not always. Nor is it necessarily our faith that decides the issue but His own larger purposes. When tragedy strikes, our first response should be to ask God what He requires of us. Faith for a miracle or trust in the face of tragedy.[3]

Most often, whether it is physical, spiritual, or emotional pain, God leads us into the trusted hands of professionals for treatment.

Mental health is on a continuum. There is no perfectly mentally healthy person, but not everyone needs counseling to solve problems and conflicts.

Conflict is not always bad, and in many situations it can be an opportunity for growth. It is when the conflict begins to interfere with normal daily function that help is needed.

Family members will notice several symptoms when a wife, husband, child, or parent is struggling and needs intervention. As he looked back on the days that led up to Elizabeth's decision to start therapy, David remembered how irritable she was.

"She was a raw nerve," he said. "She would burst into tears if I looked at her sideways. Or she would fly off the handle over the stupidest things—like when the mail was late. Oh, how I prayed the mail would arrive on time. She was easily distracted and couldn't make a decision to save her life. It was awful."

For others, behavior turns inward. They will not respond to questions, and exhibit little or no feeling over everyday events or even crises. They will stare into space a lot, and lose interest in things that once brought pleasure. Their appetite may disappear and their personal hygiene be neglected.

As frightening and distasteful as it might be, you need to look for signs of suicide. Don't be afraid to ask. Most people want you to ask. Asking will not plant a seed of self-destruction. To quote Karl Menninger:

> There are certain subjects about which we speak often in jest as if to forestall the necessity of ever discussing them seriously. Suicide is one of them. So great is the taboo on suicide that some people will not even say the word, some newspapers will not print accounts of it and even scientists have avoided it as a subject of research.[4]

(In the Appendix at the back of this book, you will find more details about suicide and what you can do in case of emergency.)

Don't run from thoughts of suicide. Even the great Prophet Elijah prayed that God would take his life.

> Then he went on alone into the wilderness, traveling all day, and sat down under a broom bush and prayed that he might die.
>
> "I've had enough," he told the Lord. "Take away my life. I've got to die sometime, and it might as well be now" (1 Kings 19:4).

The Tears Don't Stop

Elizabeth sat on the edge of her bed. She looked around the room as she fought with feelings of trepidation and sadness. Although she knew every flower on the wallpaper and every spot that collected the most dust, she felt alienated and frightened as though she no longer belonged in her own bedroom and the bedroom no longer belonged to her.

I wish the kids were home, she thought. *It's so quiet, too quiet.* It was the first time she could remember wanting to hear the sounds of the kids fighting, the stereo blaring. But it would be hours before anyone came home.

"Well," she said. "I've got to do something." Elizabeth walked to her dresser. Although she knew the tears would start again, she felt compelled to look at the pictures of her family as though it was for the very last time.

As she held Daniel's baby picture, she felt a rush of anxiety and tears she couldn't explain. She felt caught in the stranglehold of a huge monster she couldn't escape. In fact, the harder she struggled against the monster's grip, the worse her symptoms grew.

She wiped her finger around the frame of her parents' wedding picture and tried to understand her confusion. Certainly she loved them. Yet at the same time she felt anger, a rage she could not explain. Again the ugly monster of depression wrapped its hands around her spirit and shook.

Elizabeth turned the picture face down on the dresser and left the room. *The tears just keep coming,* she thought. *They just keep coming.*

Elizabeth's tears were draining her emotional and physical energy. By midday she had no strength left, and the only solace she could find was in sleep.

Depression and anxiety were taking their toll on Elizabeth and her family. This kind of conflict was no longer something she could handle by herself, or over a cup of coffee with her husband or a close friend.

Elizabeth's mental health had dipped deeply in the direction of emotional illness. The only way to effectively fight the monster was to stop struggling alone and reach out for help.

In his book, *His Image . . . My Image,* Josh McDowell compares the resurrection of Lazarus with the process of therapy. Lazarus had been dead four days. He was wrapped in the garments of death, linen wrappings soaked in spices to preserve the body. Then Jesus commanded the corpse to come alive.

When Lazarus walked out of the tomb, he no longer needed his death garments. But they were not instantly, supernaturally peeled away. Jesus told Lazarus' friends, "Unwrap him and let him go" (John 11:44). With help, the layers of linen were taken off and Lazarus was free to experience new life.[5]

In a similar way, the process of counseling unwinds the old wrappings of a distorted self-image, with the help of a professional.

Chapter Three
Hidden Colors

Michelangelo painted the ceiling of the Sistine Chapel nearly 500 years ago. Over the centuries the brilliance of his masterpiece had been hidden away behind layers of candle soot and dirt. The discoloration and subsequent darkening of the ceiling had become so pronounced that it led one archeologist of the late 1700s to declare Michelangelo as "the greatest of all draftsmen and weakest colorist."[1]

In 1980 a group of historians, artists, and craftsmen set about the task of cleaning the fresco. Their results were surprising and at times awe-inspiring. The craftsmen uncovered riches of color they never expected.

After nearly a decade of painstaking work, it was the

little toe on Jonah's right foot that felt the final swipe of the sponge from the Vatican's chief restorer. At last, no longer blanketed under dirt and grime, Jonah and everyone else glowed with health and vibrance.[2]

The process was slow and arduous. Only with steady and progressive work was the team able to bring Michelangelo's work back to its original brilliance.

Each of us is one of God's masterful designs. Because of sin, various forms of abuse, struggles, or mental illness, many people have lost the colors and brilliance God intended. But the colors need not be lost forever.

Like the Sistine Chapel restorers, the counselor works to clean away symptoms and behaviors caused by years of struggle or illness that have discolored a person's true self.

Also like the restorers, the counselor's work is slow. It is done with great care, patience, understanding, and respect.

Therapy is a process that allows a person to become aware of inner wounds and battles . . . wounds left open and unhealed, battles unresolved and still raging.

Using techniques of listening and questioning, the therapist helps the client put into words the feelings and thoughts associated with these wounds and conflicts. Within the close comfort of the client/counselor environment, pain can be faced head-on.

Through naming the wounds and talking about the pain, the war-weary soldiers of the battle are finally put to rest. Then, the person is free to change, to make choices, and to see him or herself, life, and God more realistically.

With all the layers of a distorted self-image removed, a person's hidden colors surface. Family members and friends can see the real person hidden beneath the grime.

First Visit

"I don't understand," sobbed Elizabeth. "The tears keep coming. I just cry over everything. I know I must be . . .

you know . . . nuts or something."

I could hear the depression in her voice. "You sound very sad," I said, "but that doesn't mean you're nuts."

First visits are very nervous times, and Elizabeth's was no exception. I could see the tension in her body language. She was tearful and fidgety. She never once made eye contact.

The most she could muster was to relate some of her symptoms, those she had already told her family physician. He used a stethoscope to listen for symptoms. I used my training, experience, and my intuition—the counselor's most important tool—to listen for trouble.

I could hear and see that something very deep lay at the root of her nightmares, depression, and panic attacks. Something was threatening the life David and Elizabeth had built. Something was putting a wedge between Elizabeth and God. Something was hiding her true colors.

Although given a clean bill of physical health, Elizabeth was in pain. She was experiencing a problem that could not be cut away with a surgeon's knife or knocked out with a course of antibiotics. Elizabeth's physical symptoms were caused by emotion.

Her emotional and physical pain, in turn, was affecting her spiritual life. Elizabeth was feeling distant from God, isolated, banished to a deserted island . . . an island so far away that her prayers were not heard.

Elizabeth was not crazy or spiritually flawed. Her connection with God and her family was temporarily blanketed behind layers of emotional turmoil and physical distress.

Three Rings

One way of visualizing Elizabeth's experience is with the following illustrations.

Everyone has three rings or spheres of influence, physical, emotional, and spiritual which are set within a nurturing environment.

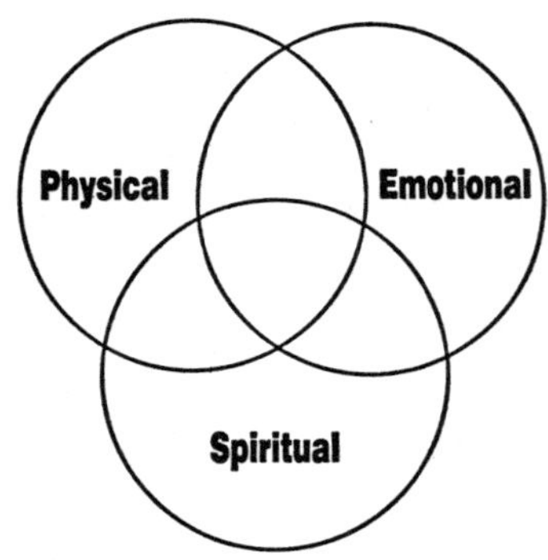

The Whole Person

God created men and women with three rings or spheres of influence set within a nurturing environment.

The Bible emphasizes the wholeness of men and women.

No ring is more important. They cannot be separated. When one ring is affected the other two are affected.

See 1 Thes. 5:23-24 and Mark 12:30-31

When one ring is damaged or distressed either by something in the nature of the physical ring, or the nurturing environment of the emotional and spiritual rings, it affects the entire person.

Psalm 6 contains a beautiful illustration of the principle. David cries out to the Lord in verse 2, "Pity me, O Lord, for I am weak. Heal me, for my body is sick."

In verse 3 he says, "I am upset and disturbed. My mind is filled with apprehension and with gloom. Oh, restore me soon." His spirit is troubled. Finally, the emotional aspect is described in verse 6, "I am worn out with pain; every night my pillow is wet with tears."

In these verses, David accurately describes the threefold way depression or any mental illness affects the entire person—body, mind, and spirit.

Watching a loved one experience pain in the physical ring is not easy or pleasant. But it is a type of pain that can be easily understood and most often accepted as real.

Spiritual Conflict

Emotional Ring
Depression
Anger
Doubt

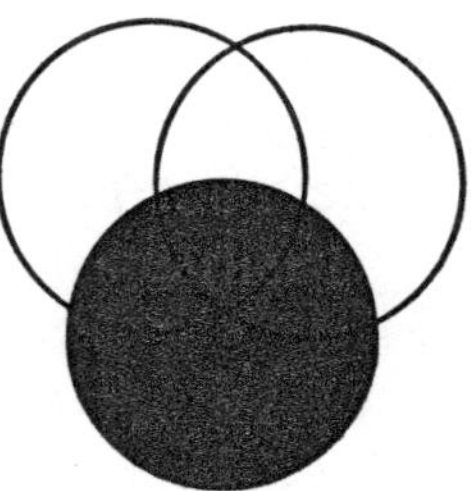

Physical Ring
Headaches
Stomach Pain
Joint Pain
Fatigue

Spiritual Ring
Doubt
Sin

Depression

Emotional Ring
Sadness
Anger
Despair
Dread

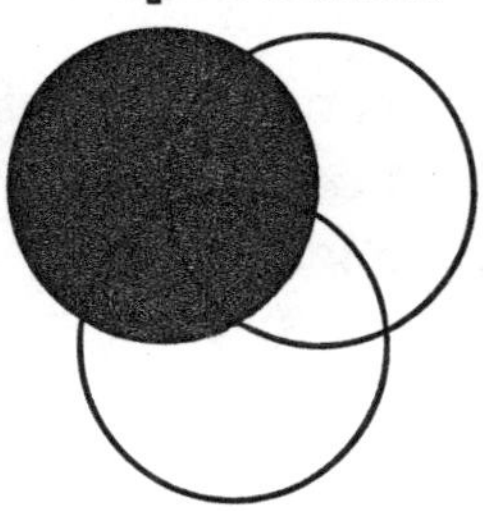

Physical Ring
Biochemical Imbalance
Poor Concentration
Sleep Disturbance
Weight Change

Spiritual Ring
Feel Abandoned by God
Loss of Interest in Church

Low Thyroid

Emotional Ring
Depression
Sadness
Anxiety

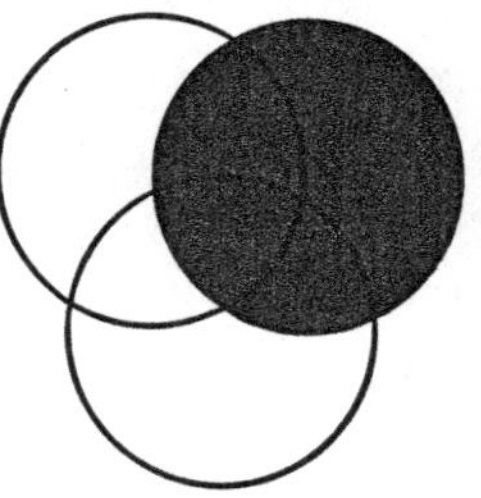

Physical Ring
Weight Loss
Coldness/Chills
Fatigue

Spiritual Ring
Distancing from God
Anger

The Accident

It was the day after Christmas. David, Elizabeth, who was then six months pregnant, and their son, Daniel, decided to take a country drive. They had traveled about an hour away from home when the accident happened on a rural stretch of highway.

Their car was struck head-on. David and Daniel received only superficial bruises. Elizabeth sustained a broken ankle and a fractured pelvis, as well as numerous bumps and bruises.

The pain that Elizabeth experienced from her physical injuries was staggering. Because of her pregnancy, she was unable to take any kind of pain medication including a simple aspirin.

"I could *see* her pain then," said David. "She shook and trembled all over. I could hear her pain when she couldn't tolerate it anymore and burst into tears. That was a pain I could handle. I knew how to comfort her then."

To Tremble Inwardly

When King David cried out to the Lord, the words he chose spoke of a pain that caused him to tremble inwardly, in places no one could see.

Although David wrote these words thousands of years ago, they are still accurate today. People experiencing emotional turmoil often describe themselves as feeling shaky inside, under the skin, deep inside their muscles.

As Elizabeth's long recovery dragged on, what was happening in the physical ring influenced the emotional and spiritual rings.

She became depressed from being confined to bed and unable to take care of her needs herself. It was hard for her to rely on others. She felt isolated and alone.

For four months Elizabeth was unable to attend church. Being absent from the fellowship was hard and threatened to pull her away from God and Bible study.

"I knew those things were happening," said David. "I could tell she was getting depressed and losing interest in church and God, but even so, I could handle it. I saw the reason for it towed to a junkyard. Every time I looked at her, at our unborn child or at Daniel, I saw that out-of-control car slam into us."

If only David could have seen Elizabeth's out-of-control father slam into her as she was growing up, it would have made her emotional recovery easier to understand.

Putting the Rings Back in Sync

When Elizabeth broke her ankle and fractured her pelvis, her three rings were pulled out of sync. It became the orthopedist's responsibility to put the physical ring back in order.

Emotional pain, just like physical pain, wrenches the rings out of harmony. Most often the damage is done in childhood and adolescence, so that people grow up with these three areas out of sync. Still, they struggle to work together in harmony as God designed.

But as we've seen with Elizabeth, the wrenching damage done in her emotional life eventually began to be felt. Symptoms developed and professional care was needed to put the rings back in order.

For the team that restored the Sistine Chapel to its original brilliance, it was a matter of computer analysis, chemical preparation, and careful inch-by-inch cleansing.

For the counselor, restoring a person's hidden colors and reestablishing balance in mind, body, and spirit is a matter of emotional analysis, talking, listening, and careful, layer-by-layer exposure of buried pain and wounds.

God has made us with the ability to explore the deepest parts of ourselves (1 Corinthians 2:11). This is a fact of God's planning and design to take comfort in. God is very much a part of the counseling process.

In his book *Putting Away Childish Things,* David Seamands writes:

> You cannot cut yourself off from your own history. You are a complex tapestry, woven with a million strands, some which reach back to Adam and beyond him to God who created you in His image. But many of the most important threads in the complex design of who you are were introduced in your childhood.[3]

Now the importance of exploring that childhood, of reaching into the past, is to see what fibers of the tapestry have been damaged and are affecting the present.

Counselors are not mining for blame or digging for fault, but are searching with the lamp of God's Spirit for responsibility to thereby unlock the shackles of the past.

It didn't take more than a couple of sessions for me to realize that Elizabeth's problems did indeed stretch back into her childhood. There were many lies and distortions that needed cleansing. There were many fibers that needed to be straightened in order to strengthen the tapestry of her life, a life that included her husband and two children.

It was going to be a difficult process—for everyone.

The Course Is Set

After her third visit, Elizabeth made the commitment to therapy. During that session we discussed goals, diagnosis, and therapeutic options. I told Elizabeth I saw five areas that needed work.

1. I saw her anxiety in trying to deal with her feelings of anger and pain.
2. I believed she suffered from a fear of success.
3. I experienced her overactive conscience. It was very punitive and self-destructive.
4. I told her I could see how much she hated herself.

5. I believed she was afraid of intimacy.

In the back of my mind, I harbored an opinion that Elizabeth might have been a victim of childhood sexual abuse. But this was something that would need to come up later, when Elizabeth was ready.

I was careful not to leave her with only negative impressions. I also pointed out the strengths I saw over the last few weeks. "You are very intelligent," I said, "and I suspect you are extremely creative. You show a sincere desire to change and an ability to look inward."

I recommended medication for both anxiety and depression. This usually is the hardest pill to swallow. But there was more going on inside of Elizabeth than just the emotional problems. The physical ring was hurting as well. The use of psychiatric drugs was aimed at restoring Elizabeth's brain chemistry to a normal physiologic state.

I often equate going through life depressed with running the Boston marathon in cement Reeboks®. A person with this handicap will never win the race. Psychiatric medication removes the concrete running shoes that have been weighing a person down. It relieves the physical symptoms of depression and anxiety, freeing the client to work out their struggles more comfortably.

Some people fear the use of drugs because of their side effects. All drugs, from antibiotics to aspirin, have side effects. It is the therapist's goal to use medication for the shortest possible time and still facilitate a cure.

Nearing the end of his life, Vincent Van Gogh wrote to his brother Theodore, "What consoles me is that I am beginning to consider madness as an illness like any other, and I accept it as such."

Elizabeth was willing to try the medication, and to go through much pain and many hours of confusion, depression, anxiety, and anger to feel better about life, and eventually to become the person hidden deep inside of her.

(For further information on the different classes of psychiatric drugs, their uses and side effects, see the Appendix.)

Depression

On her next visit we talked about depression and what it meant for Elizabeth to suffer.

"Depression is a thief," she said. "It is robbing me of everything I hold dear. I don't enjoy my life, my family, my God. I can't love anymore."

"I used to notice everything," she continued, "the way colors changed after a rainfall, the first crocuses of spring. But now I don't care. I loved music—classical to jazz, but it all sounds the same now. I feel like this monster has squashed the very life out of me."

Depression, anxiety, mental illness are diseases not just of the mind but of the heart, a word Scripture uses to describe the very center of our being, the core of existence.

DEPRESSION

More than an occasional
bout with the blues

It is an all-consuming and sustained feeling of despair, hopelessness, and worthlessness.

SYMPTOMS INCLUDE:

- Sleep disturbance
- Loss of appetite
- Fatigue
- Hyperactivity or slowed behavior
- Loss of interest in life
- Decreased sex drive
- Difficulty concentrating and making decisions
- Recurrent thoughts of death or suicide

God does not look on outward beauty or ugliness. He looks deep into the heart, the taproot of all our pains and pleasures, our hopes and dreams. When a human heart, designed to hold so much is shattered, it takes a gentle, tender touch to piece it back together.

This is the calling of the counselor and the loved one—to mend a broken heart. Although he would not journey on the same road with his wife, David would walk a parallel path that would allow him as much involvement as he desired and was clinically possible.

So often people say that seeing is believing. Without some tangible proof or personal experience, a shadow of doubt hovers in our minds. That is one reason spouses or loved ones find the process of recovery so difficult to understand.

Earlier we saw how effectively David was able to comfort and support Elizabeth after their car accident. He had experienced the actual crash and could easily identify with her pain.

Now he was asked to believe in a process he couldn't see, in pain he had no connection with. No X ray would show him the misaligned warp and woof of the tapestry of Elizabeth's life.

David was also making a tremendous commitment. He had entrusted his wife's heart into someone else's hands. For David and Elizabeth, believing would come before seeing.

W.P. Inge (1860–1954), Dean of St. Paul's Cathedral in London, said, "Faith begins as an experiment and ends as an experience." For this family it was an experiment that would succeed.

Chapter Four
A Relationship of Trust

QUESTION ONE: What kind of relationship begins, grows, and ends in secret? Usually takes place in one room with the door securely closed, on preplanned days, for a very specific period of time, and is, by nature, incredibly lopsided?

ANSWER: The client/therapist relationship.

QUESTION TWO: How can anything that sounds so self-limiting not only thrive, but incorporate many of the same qualities of any other close relationship?

ANSWER: This is not answered as simply as Question One. By this we do not mean it is impossible to understand this relationship. We just mean that there are no easy answers to adequately define what occurs in a therapeutic session.

It may take some time for you to fully accept this new connection that your wife or husband or other loved one has made.

The Battle

In Shakespeare's *Hamlet,* King Claudius said, "When sorrows come, they come not as a single spy, but in battalions."[1] Persons enter therapy with great, strong armies of troubling thoughts marching through their minds. Marching without rest.

They come with problems and conflicts that have been hanging onto their hearts, like barnacles on a ship, weighing life down and interfering with day-to-day routine.

Home is not always the safest place to wage war against emotional enemies or relive an abusive, lonely, or otherwise painful past.

It is often much wiser to fight these battles in a safe place, away from family members and friends. It is also wise for those on the other side of the therapist's door to learn about the process, to find support from friends and family, and to know what to do when the battle hits home.

In Part Two we will discuss specific ways family members and friends can find support and also be supportive during this time. For now, let's take a look behind the closed door of the counselor's office and see just what makes this relationship so unique and special.

The Safe Haven

There are as many types of counseling and counselors as there are fast-food restaurants. It is not the purpose of this book to discuss all the available techniques. Our intention is to look at the essential building blocks that are common to all schools of thought.

(For a list of these therapeutic techniques, and an explanation of their basic working mechanisms, see the Appendix.)

In order for the process to be successful, the counselor or therapist needs to create an environment in which the client feels safe and free to explore his or her deepest thoughts and feelings.

When the psalmist says that he will put his *trust* in God, he is, in essence, saying he will first run to God, take refuge or hide with God, confide in and lean on Him for comfort.

Fortunately God is big enough to be available to all of us, all of the time. But keep in mind a story about a little girl who was afraid of the dark. Her mother told her that she wasn't alone, that Jesus was with her. Although the little girl appreciated her mother's words, she still said, "I need someone with skin."

In many ways, the Christian counselor becomes Jesus with skin, a real live person to run to, take refuge with, confide in, and lean on for comfort and support. That is the definition of *trust,* the cornerstone on which the client/counselor relationship rests.

Trust does not just happen. A patient does not immediately believe in the trustworthiness of the counselor. As with any close relationship, this one needs time to grow and consistency to thrive.

It should be emphasized that no doctor or counselor can promise perfection. A good counselor will make a commitment to do his or her best, acknowledge mistakes when they happen, and work to correct any hurt or damage.

Any child growing up in a troubled home learns four very damaging rules.

DON'T FEEL
DON'T TALK
DON'T TRUST
DON'T NEED

A person in therapy is being asked to break these rules.

And since this code of conduct is learned in childhood, generally from parents, it is the hardest to crack, the hardest to change.

That is why trust is the most important aspect of the client/therapist relationship. Patients must be able to trust in order to freely feel and discuss their deepest longings, fears, and pains. And then allow themselves to need a therapist in ways they might have needed Mother or Father, Sister or Brother.

How Does a Counselor Become Trustworthy?

There are four building blocks that the counselor places on the cornerstone of trust.

- RELIABILITY. The physical reliability of the counselor is essential. He or she has the responsibility to be on time for appointments, to make phone calls when promised, and to respect the time given to the client.
- EMPATHY. Empathy is not the same as sympathy. Sympathy says, "I want to feel exactly the way you feel. I want to claim your pain as my own." Sympathy can have condescending tones, attempting to negate the uniqueness of the sufferer's pain, thus leaving the person alone.

Empathy goes far beyond feeling. The empathetic listener, although moved by a person's pain, tries to understand *how* those feelings are experienced. The empathetic counselor is willing to walk in another's shoes and see the world from the client's perspective, at the same time adding clarity to those feelings.

- VULNERABILITY. Closely associated with empathy is the therapist's willingness to be vulnerable. The therapist does not come to sessions behind a professional facade. She is not playing a role or being phony. She is "for real," an honest-to-goodness person with feelings, needs, and history, and has the courage to risk hurt and deep feeling.

Training, experience in working with people, knowledge of how the mind functions, and how an individual sense of self develops allow the therapist to be vulnerable, and to absorb the client's feelings without getting overwhelmed.

• RESPECT. We have all heard that we are to love the sinner but not the sin. This is what the therapist does. The therapist cares for, values, and treasures the client without judgment, criticism, or ridicule.

The therapist does not lay aside her values or morality during a session. Yet she accepts the client for who she is, the way she is. In this way, the therapist echoes the biblical truth that grace is free and cannot be earned. God gives His love to every person, in every situation.

The Art of Listening

If trust is the cornerstone of the safe haven, then the art of listening is the mortar that holds it all together and makes it work.

"It was the first time in my life that I felt truly, completely listened to," said Elizabeth. "It was as though the doctor was able to reach out and grab hold of my every word, even my every sigh, and cradle them in her heart.

"There, with the light of God that I knew was inside of her, she looked at my words. And then, the most remarkable thing of all, she returned them to me in a way that added clarity, enabling me to find answers or at least to know where to look. I felt as though I finally mattered, even to someone as important as herself."

Perhaps this feeling of what makes the client/counselor relationship so special was best described by novelist George Eliot:

> Oh the comfort, the inexpressible comfort of feeling safe with a person; having neither to weigh thoughts nor measure words but to pour them all out, just as it

> is, chaff and grain together, knowing that a faithful hand will take and sift them, keep what is worth keeping and then, with the breath of kindness blow the rest away.[2]

"The more I talked and she listened, the easier it became to let her hear the most painful words. Even when my words were punctuated with tears, cloudbursts of tears, she didn't flinch. She stayed with me. Once or twice she even cried with me."

That is what people in pain want and need most of all, not only from a counselor but from a listening spouse or friend—that we stay with them in their pain.

Confidentiality

We have already explored the major building blocks of the safe haven. Confidentiality is the shield around the safe haven that protects the client from further emotional hurt.

There are both emotional and legal aspects to confidentiality. On the emotional side, the therapist is morally and ethically bound to hold whatever is said or done in the therapeutic setting in confidence.

The wisdom of confidentiality is seen in Scripture. "A gossip betrays a confidence, but a trustworthy man keeps a secret" (Proverbs 11:13, NIV). And according to Proverbs 18:8, "The words of a gossip are like choice morsels; they go down to a man's innermost parts" (NIV).

The words that tell of a wounded, painful past do not come easy. Often a client will feel embarrassed or ashamed of the treatment they received as a child, or of things that they might have said and done.

Theologian George Fuller says that we all have our own sacred ground of suffering, and we don't let just anyone tread on that soil.

The therapist understands this and knows that as clients

give language and life to their pain, they are not freely offering their past for the therapist to use outside the sanctuary of the office.

"But Why Can't She Tell Me?"

"David seems upset today," said Elizabeth. "He's wondering how I can come here and tell you all kinds of stuff and not him. I think he feels left out."

"What did you tell him?" I asked.

"Nothing really. I guess I'm not sure why I can't tell him everything. He is my husband. I know he loves me and wouldn't ever repeat things, even to his best friend. But I just don't want to tell him everything."

Elizabeth and I sat in silence for a moment. It is often in these silences that a client can find answers to questions, or finally put a face with a particular pain or memory.

"Well," she said, "it's hard enough telling you this stuff. It hurts."

"What do you think would happen if you told David?"

"I'm not so sure he'd understand. Not the way you do. Maybe he wouldn't love me anymore."

This is a concern of just about everyone who does therapy. In truth, a spouse or family member or even a close friend will probably continue to love them just as deeply. But because clients are struggling with issues of self-esteem and self-love, they feel an overpowering fear of rejection if anyone learns the truths they are facing.

As therapy progresses and clients begin to feel more comfortable with their past, their feelings and themselves, they will find it easier to open up and let loved ones in.

Transference

It happens not just between a client and counselor but everywhere, in all kinds of relationships. How often we have heard the words, "Don't take it out on me!" "Leave your problems at the office." "Don't be angry with the kids just because you're upset with me." Anyone can be the target of another's transferred feelings.

Take Stacy, for example, the young woman behind the counter at the local video store. In walks a seemingly rational person. He approaches nineteen-year-old Stacy whose only crime is that she's working her way through college.

The man asks Stacy if she has a particular movie. She searches the computer.

"I'm sorry," she says. "We have it, but they're all out."

The man grimaces and snaps at Stacy.

"What do you mean . . . all out? I've been waiting six months to see that movie. How can they be all gone? Didn't you buy enough?"

Stacy stammers and recoils from the mean and unreasonable man. She apologizes again; but he doesn't hear or care. He just storms out of the store.

Stacy watches as he motions to his wife, opens the car door, angrily shoos the dog into the backseat, slams the door, then slaps the steering wheel.

In this scene everyone caught it—Stacy, his wife, the dog, even the car. This is transference in action. If we could catch up with this man and talk with him, we would discover that the roots of his anger reached deep into his subconscious mind. This was where he unconsciously buried the anger and frustration he felt toward people in his past. Acting his anger out in the video store helped him blow off steam. It did nothing to resolve the hurts of the past.

But when this kind of anger and frustration is brought into the safe haven of the therapist's office, it is considered a normal part of the therapy process. The therapist is trained to look beyond the outward emotional display and help clients figure out the true target of their feelings.

Anger is not the only feeling that gets buried. Feelings

associated with loss, fear, abandonment, and guilt can be unconsciously relived over and over. It is not until the true source of those feelings is discovered that any resolution is found.

Transference is threatening because it involves getting in touch with those feelings and discovering their source. But by taking the experienced hand of the therapist, a patient is able to walk into the past and place those thoughts and feelings at the root.

Transference can also happen in our relationship with God. As a child Elizabeth was often abandoned by a too-busy father, severely punished for the slightest misdeed, and told that her feelings were insignificant.

As an adult she "transferred" the feelings she had about her father onto God. She could not see God as a loving father, with outstretched arms ready to love and encourage her. She saw a fierce, angry God always ready to punish.

It was not only God that Elizabeth saw as punitive and unloving; she also saw me in that light. Although I reassured her countless times, she was still convinced that I would abandon her, punish her, and someday tell her that all her feelings were insignificant.

Because of my training and experience, I was able to absorb Elizabeth's feelings and work with them. I knew that she would eventually see that it was not me or God she was angry with, but her father.

Transference is one of the dynamics of therapy that makes it such a close and intense relationship.

A Three-legged Race

Listen to Elizabeth's words when I asked her to explain what it meant to be in relationship with me.

"It's like a physical, emotional, and spiritual three-legged race. I feel bound to you, supported by you, and spiritually connected to you as we go on to the finish line.

"When I stumble, you fall with me. Sometimes it's your energy that picks us up; sometimes we lean on each other for balance. When I stray off course, when our one bound leg gets turned around and wants to go the other way, you gently pull us back on course.

"Even though there is a lot of stumbling, falling down, and getting back up, I feel as long as you stay close and walk or run with me, I'll get to the finish line. I'll get better.

"I never believed my parents loved me. Maybe they did but couldn't show it because of their own histories. In any case, it still hurt. I grew up alone, with no one to really listen to me or guide me. I had to keep all my feelings stuffed inside at a time when I was most vulnerable. I couldn't defend myself from verbal and physical attacks. I couldn't even cry without fear of more hurt. But now, sitting here with you, when I remember my father coming after me like an out-of-control car on an icy hill, I don't hide my feelings. Finally the child inside can cry."

PART 2

Chapter Five
Being Real and Feeling Important

"Where have you been?" demanded David. "You were supposed to be home an hour ago."

"I'm sorry," said Elizabeth. "The session ran over and then I needed to be alone for a while."

"Alone?" questioned David. "While I've been here with the kids? I was worried. I thought something might have happened."

Elizabeth hung her jacket and handbag in the closet. David watched her movements. They were slow, very deliberate. He felt as though he was watching an instant replay.

"Hi honey," Elizabeth said, patting Anna on the head. "I'm sorry I'm late."

"Oh, great!" shouted David. "You hug Anna, tell her

you're sorry. What about me? I wish you would just snap out of this . . . this stupid depression, anxiety thing. It's starting to depress me."

"I said I was sorry. You just weren't listening. It was a rough session."

David's mind began to fill with all kinds of questions and doubts about what Elizabeth was doing. It all seemed so secretive, so removed from himself.

"It just seems that you would rather be with that doctor than with me. What can she do that I can't?"

"She can listen."

David shouted, "Listen? If that's all you need, I can listen."

Elizabeth cried, "You don't understand. It's not the same kind of listening."

"You're right I don't understand. She's coming between us. It's like I don't matter. You tell her everything and me nothing."

"It's because you matter so much," sobbed Elizabeth.

Elizabeth turned and walked into the kitchen. David fell into the sofa with a thud. *She's the one seeing the shrink. How come I feel so lousy?*

Feeling Left Out

Elizabeth was well into the course of her therapy. But what began as a once, sometimes twice-a-week visit, now turned into a three-times-a-week ordeal for her husband.

Left behind to care for their increasingly demanding children several hours a week, David was beginning to feel left out, shut out, and tuned out.

At first he looked forward to the extra time with his kids. "It will be great," he smiled. "We can bond."

Now David dreaded her sessions. He never knew what kind of mood she would be in when she got home. Even nonappointment days were difficult. David just did not know how to act around Elizabeth. He was afraid of setting off an emotional time bomb he felt certain was ticking away inside of her.

David tried to be supportive. He didn't like the anger he felt toward Elizabeth, and he felt guilty because he couldn't stop. He didn't like the anger he held toward me, but he didn't know what to do with it. I was no longer a home-healer in his eyes. I had become a home-wrecker.

David was experiencing a very common reaction of a person who loves someone in therapy. He was riding a seesaw. One day he was up, pleased that Elizabeth recognized she needed help and was willing to go through the painful steps of recovery. He also knew that just as Elizabeth needed to trust me, he was called to do the same.

On another day he was down. David wanted to be the one to help his wife through her problems. He could not understand why his love was not powerful enough to make her better. He felt helpless and useless.

But David, and all those who love someone in pain, have within themselves some very powerful, healing gifts to give their loved ones.

Becoming Real

How many times have we heard someone ask, "Is this for real?" or "Are you for real?" Or how about, "I can't believe this is really happening to me."

For someone experiencing emotional pain, particularly the pain associated with depression and anxiety, the question of what is real and what is not can be perplexing and frightening.

Some people have even described themselves as feeling unreal when the maelstrom of depression and/or anxiety is at its strongest. Why does the mind do this? Clinically we know that this feeling of unreality is one way the mind attempts to distance itself from hurtful feelings and stresses.

What does it mean to be real? Being real means that something or someone is not imaginary, fictional, or pretended. A person, object, or even a disease is authentic and genuine. When people are in pain, their questions of what is real and what is not must be answered delicately.

First, as silly as it may sound, they must be assured that *they are real.* And second, that *what they are experiencing is really happening to them.*

Several years ago Elizabeth's father made a trip to the Holy Land. While he was there, he purchased a small oil lamp used thousands of years ago to light a nomad family's tent.

Along with the lamp came a letter from the museum attesting to its authenticity and genuineness. It was a real lamp used by real people. But what exactly made this small, clay lamp real? Was it the letter from the museum curator? Or was it made real by the hands that dug the earth and molded and shaped the clay into a usable vessel?

When a young mind is first molded and shaped by hands that don't have the tools to love and nurture in healthy ways, the results can be poor self-esteem, loneliness, depression, or severe mental illness.

An unhealthy nurturing environment leaves children with searing thoughts of unreality . . . thoughts that tell them that they are not genuine. They grow up with a belief system that convinces them they are not lovable, even to God.

Putting the "Real" into Practice

The potter can take an unlovely, unusable piece of clay and reshape it into a work of beauty and strength. This is the goal of therapy. You can help to achieve this goal for your loved one by being *real.*

Hidden within this simple word *real* are the powerful, healing gifts you inherited from God, gifts that you can offer to your loved one in pain.

- RESPECT. If we wanted to fit the definition and wisdom of respect into a Chinese fortune cookie, the little slip of paper would read, "Love the sinner but not the sin." However, respect involves much more than will ever fit inside a fortune cookie.

Respect looks past outward behavior and words to the heart. People in emotional pain already feel embarrassed, ashamed, even dirty. They don't need a spotlight flooding their condition. While unsatisfactory behavior is not condoned, words of correction should be wrapped in love.

● ENCOURAGEMENT. When we give the gift of encouragement to another person, we are actively participating in their journey toward self-awareness, self-assuredness, and significance.

In the book *Encouragement: The Key to Caring,* Larry Crabb and Dan Allender cite a key passage in Hebrews to define our second gift. They say that the Greek word for encouragement literally means "to stir up, to provoke, to incite people in a given direction."[1] These are powerful words that must be tempered with kindness and knowledge of a person's strengths and limitations.

Don't worry if your words are not accepted all at once. Remember, your job is not to rescue and make it all better. Encouragement is a process, a gradual building up of another's self-esteem.

For someone in recovery, sometimes the most encouraging words they can hear are, "I love you, I admire what you are doing, and I know you will get better."

● ACCEPTANCE. Acceptance is a lot like respect because it involves a nonjudgmental attitude. Acceptance does not hurry people along on their journey. It accepts them wherever they are along the road, even if they have been stuck in a ditch for a long time.

Acceptance finds a way to be comfortable in your loved one's world. The psalmist paints a beautiful picture of the way God accepts us, and knows us just for who we are.

"He is like a father to us, tender and sympathetic. . . . For He knows we are but dust, and that our days are few and brief, like grass, like flowers" (Psalm 103:13-14).

• LISTENING. Of all the gifts we have to offer, listening is the most precious. When Solomon became King of Israel, God appeared to him in a dream and told him to ask for anything he wanted and it would be given to him. Solomon could have asked for a long life, or for great riches. He did not. Rather, he asked for a listening heart so that he could rule well and know right from wrong (1 Kings 3:9).

When a person struggling through the labyrinth of emotional illness asks someone to listen, he or she is probably not asking for quick solutions and advice. Most likely your loved one is just asking that you hear his words, see her tears, and stay tuned in with his thoughts. Abide awhile with his or her pain, even if it brings tears of your own. How precious it is to have someone to cry alongside of you.

Listening then becomes an agent of healing. When a person feels truly listened to, they feel loved, accepted, respected, and important.

So don't squirm and become anxious as you listen. Don't search for just the right words. There may not be any at that moment. But extend your listening ear to the still, small voice of the Lord. He will give you the proper words at the proper time.

Respect Encourage Accept Listen	What it means to be real

We Still Need Boundaries

Watching a loved one wrestle with the invisible armies of emotional illness can leave you feeling helpless and frustrated. No matter how *real* you have been, your loved one remains unchanged. Becoming real, in the sense of knowing oneself and one's true strengths and weaknesses, takes time.

Consider this passage from Margery Williams' children's classic *The Velveteen Rabbit:*

> "Real isn't how you are made," said the Skin Horse. "It's a thing that happens to you. When a child loves you for a long, long time, not just to play with, but *really* loves you, then you become Real."
>
> "Does it hurt?" asked the Rabbit.
>
> "Sometimes," said the Skin Horse, for he was always truthful. "When you are Real you don't mind being hurt."
>
> "Does it happen all at once, like being wound up," he asked, "or bit by bit?"
>
> "It doesn't happen all at once," said the Skin Horse. "You become. It takes a long time. Generally, by the time you are Real, most of your hair has been loved off, and your eyes drop out and you get loose in the joints and very shabby. But these things don't matter at all, because once you are Real you can't be ugly, except to people who don't understand."[2]

In the meantime, there are things you can do to keep some sense of normalcy and order. If you are supporting someone who is struggling with depression, insist that he or she showers regularly, eats healthy foods, and completes certain tasks—even if it's just taking out the trash.

Encourage your loved one to follow "doctor's orders," e.g., take medicine on time, go to counseling sessions.

Some therapy techniques ask the client to keep a journal or draw pictures. It's a good idea to stay interested, even if you're not allowed to read a diary or see a picture. You're still helping by voicing your interest.

Setting limits does not apply only to the client. You have to set boundaries for yourself. Boundaries in relationships are what distinguish one person from another. Boundaries enforce autonomy and separateness in a positive way, allowing each person to have pride in self-ownership.

Don't try to talk yourself into believing that you don't have needs, or that you can "take" everything that's thrown your way. Admit when you are tired, frustrated, angry, or when you feel a boundary has been crossed. Take breaks. Find someone to talk with. Don't allow yourself to be dragged down by another's depression or problems, no matter how much you love that person.

"I Just Can't Tell You"

David walked into the kitchen where Elizabeth was busy stirring a pot of soup. She looked preoccupied as she stared into the bubbling broth. David had seen this faraway look countless times. He stood at the doorway for several minutes before Elizabeth noticed him.

"Hi," he said. "Have a nice trip?"

Elizabeth put the wooden spoon on the counter. "Trip?" she questioned. "What are you talking about?"

David crossed his arms tightly against his chest. "I've been standing here waiting for you to come out of your fog. Where were you?"

Elizabeth took a deep, troubled breath. She sat at the table and nervously played with the saltshaker. "Just thinking . . . about things."

"So tell me. What things?"

Elizabeth adjusted her glasses and pushed some stray hairs behind her ears. "I can't," she said. "I just can't tell you."

David snapped, "Oh, fine! But you can tell the doctor, right?"

Elizabeth took more deep breaths. "David, I've tried to explain this before. It's not you. It's not that I don't want to tell you. I can't."

David walked away. Again the specter of rejection haunted him. Again he felt he wasn't good enough to hear his wife's problems.

Clients often experience emotional issues as shameful or bad. They will feel embarrassed as memories surface. It is hard enough to admit certain experiences to themselves, or to a counselor. Imagine divulging such shameful experiences to someone you live with.

One of the most common fears a therapist hears is, "If he really knew me, he wouldn't love me." This fear creates a distance that is difficult for loved ones to understand.

Withholding information is *not* keeping secrets. It is not malicious, nor is it a judgment on another person's adequacy to love and relate.

In many ways, the safe haven of the therapist's office is a proving ground for certain feelings and experiences. In time a client will move toward more openness, once the truth is confronted.

Before that time comes, remember to respect, encourage, and accept your loved one *now*. There will be time and opportunity enough in the future to listen and learn.

"If You Won't Tell Me, Then I'll Ask the Doctor!"

This is not always a good idea. In the previous chapter we saw how confidentiality works as a shield to protect the client from further injury. There are also legal aspects to confidentiality.

Telephoning the therapist is not always inappropriate. Sometimes it helps to hear a comforting voice. But be aware that the therapist is bound by law not to divulge the details of what is said and done in the office. And expect the therapist to tell the client that you called and what you said.

How open the door to the therapist's office is to a spouse or family member hinges on three key issues:

1. The severity of the patient's condition. In cases of severe personality disorders such as schizophrenia or manic-depression, it is important that the doctor has a person close to the patient to work with as a liaison.

Family members and friends need to know what to look for and what safeguards they can take to protect themselves and the patient.

2. The patient's wishes of how extensively another may be involved. This is something that may change frequently throughout the therapy process.

3. The therapist's clinical judgment. In cases of attempted or even threatened suicide, homicide, and suspected child abuse, the therapist becomes bound by another set of laws that requires she inform authorities and family.

Any writer of children's stories and fairy tales will tell you that it is the hero's lot in life to go it alone. No matter how many wise and wonderful people go along on the journey, the hero still must climb the craggy cliff alone, reach for the brass ring alone, sit inside the belly of a whale alone. For it is during these times of aloneness that growth happens, wisdom is found, and truth and beauty are discovered.

But as the hero in any story will tell you, the quest would never have been finished without the wise and wonderful people cheering him on.

Chapter Six
Shhh, Don't Tell. It's a Secret!

Kids cannot keep a secret. No matter how much you beg, promise, or threaten, it is inevitable that Mom's surprise birthday party will not surprise anyone.

So skilled are kids at spilling the beans that not only the party will be common knowledge, but also the date, time, place, and cost of the event.

Sadly, though, there are family secrets that children are very skilled at keeping . . . secrets like substance addiction, crime, child abuse, and incest . . . secrets that damage and even destroy lives and families. These secrets should not be kept; but for many reasons they slip under cracks in the floor, slink into closets, or worse, they become buried or repressed in a child's subconscious mind—the place where the most awful damage is done.

It is there, deep within the child's mind, that secrets eat away at a budding self-image, and the child is left alone to devise coping methods, build defense mechanisms, and construct fortresses to keep anyone from finding out who he really is and where he really came from.

These secrets are not fun. They are not fun to keep or to tell. But even the most well-guarded secrets have a way of springing leaks. Sometimes the leaks go unnoticed, and sometimes they cannot be ignored.

Think about the damage that can be done when a leaky roof is ignored or poorly patched. The roof may hold for a short while, but eventually it will cave in. Then you have an even bigger, more expensive problem to fix.

In just such a way, Elizabeth crashed. The secrets that were buried deep in her heart started leaking out through nightmares, anxiety, and depression. Although it took over two years of intensive therapy, the weakness in the dam finally burst and the secrets came out—sometimes in little drips, sometimes great gushes.

"When I think about this part of therapy," Elizabeth said later, "I'm reminded of the time I visited Hoover Dam. It was incredibly scary, but I wanted to explore it. I had never been so close to something as huge and awesome as that. We first went on an elevator that started going down, down, down—it seemed like forever.

"When we piled out of that little box, there we were inside Hoover Dam. We wandered along passageways—halls are what the guides called them. I was so scared. The walls leaked! Here I was thousands of feet below the ground, under tons and tons of water, and the walls leaked. I was certain they would crash. But the guides assured us that we were perfectly safe. The walls leaked for a good reason, and it was normal. Well, I don't know how normal it is to have leaking walls a mile below the ground, but I was never so glad to see the light of day."

Elizabeth's trip through Hoover Dam is a great picture of what it's like to explore inside a person's subconscious mind. A dam is an excellent way of describing the type of fortress constructed to keep the secrets hidden or submerged away from anyone else. But the secrets always leak out. And just like Hoover Dam needed to have a certain amount of leaky water, so do our minds. The leaks help us pinpoint our problems.

Most people think about the subconscious as being deep inside, buried in the mind or heart. The thing to remember about Elizabeth's experience at Hoover Dam is that she began her trip with no real knowledge of what awaited her below the surface of the ground.

After traveling for what seemed like thousands of feet and tunneling through dirt and rock-lined walls, she came out into the light. This is the stuff of therapy—going through hidden hallways looking for the light—the truth.

The therapeutic setting is a safe place to tell secrets and allow feelings to be experienced or re-experienced. The counselor is trained to absorb those feelings and discuss the terrible truths that have been hidden for so long.

When the secrets finally reach the light of day, they usually remain with the therapist until the client is strong enough to carry them home. Before this is possible, the secrets may need to be talked about over and over and over again with the therapist.

It is in this way that the client will be able to keep the secrets from resubmerging. She has an opportunity to name the pain and then claim it as truth, and develop a sense of self-confidence in what she believes.

She will also learn ways of telling her spouse or friend, sometimes even role-playing the moment. Then she will be strong enough to carry them home. This is what happened with Elizabeth. She discovered buried memories of childhood incest. For months she struggled with the truth, until she was finally able to accept the awful reality and place responsibility where it belonged.

"I Can't Believe It!"

"No!" shouted David, rising to his feet. "I don't believe you. How could such a thing happen? You told me you had never been with anyone else but me. You lied!"

Elizabeth felt the sting of David's words. Each one was like an icy snowball smacking her in the face. "I didn't lie," she cried. "I didn't know. I didn't remember. And it's not like I was unfaithful."

"How, how could you not remember something as . . . as awful as . . . " David stopped mid-sentence. "I can't even say the words."

"Raped by my uncle when I was nine. Many times."

This time David felt the sting of Elizabeth's words. "But he's my friend," said David. "We go fishing. We talk. I can't believe what you're telling me. He seems so . . . so normal."

Elizabeth knew that when she finally told David her secret, he would need time to experience his own feelings about it. Because of the friendship David and her uncle had developed, he would have a difficult time believing the truth. She knew that like most prosurvivors, David would feel a strong need to take action—to avenge his wife.

This is not an unusual reaction for someone in David's shoes. First he felt utter disbelief, then betrayal, not only by his friend but by his wife. Then he felt angry—so angry he had fantasies of murdering his wife's uncle.

"At first I just didn't want to believe it," said David. "How could any guy have sex with his own niece? And why would any girl let him do it? The whole thing disgusted me. And then, even if I did believe it, what was I supposed to do about it? I didn't sleep for a week. All I could think about was this guy, my friend, another man, with my wife. Then I had thoughts about using him as bait the next time we went fishing. The whole thing really rattled me.

"I just could not understand how she could remember the way her father beat her, but not remember something as terrible as incest. But now I know that was precisely why she repressed it. It was so terrible her young mind could not handle it."

David was not unique. It was much easier to hear about physical or verbal abuse. Incest, rape, sexual molestation of a child is such a heinous crime that we do not want to even hear about it.

This was one of the times during Elizabeth's therapy that David came to see me. I was able to help him understand that his denial of what happened to Elizabeth was similar to Elizabeth repressing the memory.

Physical abuse is terrible. Verbal abuse is terrible. Neglect, abandonment—they are all terrible. But sexual abuse is *very* terrible. It is so morally wrong we want to push it aside and pretend it never happened, just as the little girl being victimized does.

What Are You Supposed to Do?

Although the example in our story is incest, the principles and thoughts that follow apply equally to most forms of abuse and secrets.

• BELIEVE YOUR LOVED ONE. It is not unusual for family secrets to remain secrets simply because no one outside of the family believed what they were told. It is just as likely that the secret, whatever it was, was so awful that the family couldn't believe it either. Or, there was a paralyzing fear of more hurt, more drinking, more fighting if the truth was told.

Sometimes the truth is kept secret because "Daddy said so," or "Mommy made me promise not to tell anyone." Some parents hold these things over their children's heads like swords, symbols of punishment. For some the threat is death.

Children of alcoholics often learn to lie about their mother or father's condition.

"Mom has the flu," said Mary, "so you can't come in. But maybe we can play at your house."

"Gee," said Sue, "your mom has the flu a lot. We always play at my house."

Mary doesn't know what to say, quickly changes the subject, and skips along to Sue's house. The truth has just been buried deeper.

Children and wives who have been physically battered learn to cover up their wounds and bruises, not only with lies, but with makeup or clothing inappropriate for the weather. It's easier to sweat under a heavy shirt than to show the world your red stripes and purple bruises.

So, when someone you love tells you about a painful past, *listen and believe.* When such people know they are being believed, it makes them feel validated. They become more real to themselves and the people close to them.

● UNDERSTAND THAT REPRESSION DOES HAPPEN. It is not just a fancy psychological term used to dismiss someone's unhealthy behavior.

"I don't understand how you could forget something like that," said David. "It doesn't make sense."

Elizabeth did forget or repress the memories of her uncle's brutal attacks. When the truth finally surfaced in therapy, it began as flashbacks, fragmented memories, until she was finally able to remember the entire ugly experience.

Children repress certain events because their minds are not mature enough to handle them. They are not little adults and cannot stand to be treated like they are. At the moment of their trauma they are flooded with a whole set of feelings—shame, embarrassment, physical pain, betrayal, fear of suffocation, and guilt.

Children tend to take the blame for the bad things that happen around them, particularly the events they don't understand or couldn't control.

When Elizabeth, David, and Daniel were in the car accident, Daniel was only three years old. Elizabeth remembered turning around to check on her son. She was surprised by Daniel's remark. "Mama," he cried, "what did I do?" Little Daniel thought he had caused the crash. That is how a child's mind works.

- ALLOW YOUR LOVED ONE TO HAVE TIME AND ROOM TO HEAL. This does not mean you are leaving the person alone to experience the pain and anger and shame. It just means that you shouldn't be surprised if they want to be alone, or don't want to talk about it. If their anger spills onto you, try not to take it personally—it's probably transference. You can learn to absorb that anger and refuse to react to it.

When painful memories are exposed, they are like reopened wounds. These wounds still need time and care to heal, not with just a superficial skin of protection but with new, healthy cells that will grow and develop, the way they were meant to.

- DO NOT LIE DOWN LIKE A DOORMAT AND GET STOMPED ON. Be aware of your own feelings and needs. Do not let anyone make you feel like a victim. Take time to care for yourself. If you're too tired to listen, say so. Sometimes you need to choose yourself over your wife or husband or friend. It's okay to set boundaries. If you become burned out, you won't be any help at all. Your own growth and well-being are important.

DO NOT CONFRONT THE OFFENDER. As unfair as it might sound, it is not your place to confront a perpetrator.

Confrontation may or may not happen. When it does, it takes special plans and carries certain concerns that the client and therapist decide will best suit the situation.

Elizabeth decided not to confront her uncle. David, on the other hand, wanted a confrontation. But because of the delicateness of the problem and the possible repercussions, they decided it would be better to just stay away from him.

This was not easy. Still, it had to be done. They also had the uncomfortable task of making certain Uncle Richard didn't repeat his crime, this time against Anna.

See your loved one as a strong survivor, not a weak victim. Remember, therapy is teaching her how to handle life in new ways. Confrontation may be one of those new ways, but it must remain the client's choice.

• DO NOT PRESSURE YOUR LOVED ONE INTO FORGIVENESS. "Forgive and forget, forgive and forget." How often have we heard those words. Life is just not that simple. Forgiveness is not a condition of or shortcut to recovery. If it is done too quickly, still painful feelings get stuffed even deeper.

The biblical word for forgiveness literally means to cancel a debt. Physical, emotional, and spiritual debts take many forms and occur in many ways. Depending on the severity of the pain inflicted, canceling these debts is not always easy. With the help and grace of Jesus Christ, forgiveness may one day be possible. Forgiveness, not forgetfulness.

Part of healing is feeling the pain, experiencing the anger, mourning the loss. If we try to zip around this part of the process and plunge into forgiveness, it won't work. It's like putting wallpaper on an unprepared surface. It sticks for a little while; but before long, sheets of paper begin peeling away from the wall, exposing the ugly paint we wanted to hide in the first place.

The goal of forgiving a person of their transgressions is

not to release them from responsibility or to cover up their sin. Forgiveness is, in a sense, the icing on the cake. It is the part of therapy that finally puts to rest the pain and hurts of the past.

Chapter Seven
Change...Is It for Better or Worse?

Anatevka was a village steeped in tradition. So steeped, in fact, that the villagers had no memory of how or why their traditions came to be. The reasons for their traditions had mostly faded into history, but the customs continued as their way of life.

Tevye, the milkman and also one of the most respected patriarchs in the village, tries to explain:

> Because of our traditions, we've kept our balance for many, many years. Here in Anatevka we have traditions for everything—how to eat, how to sleep, how to wear clothes. For instance, we always keep our heads covered and always wear a little prayer shawl.

> This shows our constant devotion to God. You may ask, how did this tradition start? I'll tell you—I don't know! But it's a tradition. Because of our traditions, everyone knows who he is and what God expects him to do.[1]

Tevye also knew one other very important point about tradition. "Without our traditions," he says, "our lives would be as shaky as—as a fiddler on the roof!"[2]

As *Fiddler on the Roof* continues, Tevye will see many of his traditions tumble, as his family and the world around them change.

Tevye believed in tradition because it held his family together, gave him a sense of security—past, present, and future. Each time he was faced with letting go of a tradition, he felt nervous and shaky. But he also had a twinkle in his eye, a look of expectancy and excitement.

So, he thought about tradition and considered change. And after arguing with himself and God, he was able to accept the change, particularly where the happiness of his daughters was concerned. Their joy and growth as individuals in their own right was more important than keeping tradition for tradition's sake.

Tevye also discovered that change did not destroy his family; in fact, they were brought closer.

Tevye accepted change as it came along, even though it meant a piece of his own identity—being the "Papa," the decision-maker—changed with it.

What Is Tradition?

We often think of tradition as custom, something we do at particular times of the year, or during events such as births and weddings.

Maybe it's traditional for your family to go to the Thanksgiving Day parade every year. Sometimes it's cold or rainy; the bleachers are hard, and there are too many people, and you would rather sleep in, but you still go—kicking and screaming all the way. Why? Because it's *tradition.*

Simply put, a tradition is something you and your family have done forever, even though nobody remembers exactly why.

There are also other kinds of traditions, those inside ourselves. These are traditions that dictate how we behave, how we respond to pain and hurt, shame and joy. Tevye held tightly to his traditions—the ones that told him how to eat, sleep, and dress, and probably how to feel.

We all want to hang on to our inward, psychological traditions just as tightly. Trying to shake loose from a negative tradition is rather like trying to shake a snapping turtle off your big toe. It's not so easy.

We have become accustomed to holding back tears and stuffing feelings inside. It is easier not to trust and to pretend we don't need any kind of emotional, spiritual, or physical help.

We abuse our children because we were abused, not consciously or in a premeditated fashion, but because it's a tradition—we can't help ourselves.

We drink because our parents did. We can't control our tempers, and so just like Daddy, we throw things and slam doors when we're angry. Or, we withdraw and don't talk, pushing the anger inside.

Elizabeth experienced both sides of this anger coin in her father. He was prone to fits of violent rage. But afterward she would see him sitting silently on the edge of his bed, withdrawn from his family. This was the anger tradition Elizabeth brought to her new family, a tradition she did not want to pass to her children.

Failure in relationships or business can be another family tradition. How sad to never reach your full potential, or accomplish the tasks God has in mind for you, because you were told you couldn't. Maybe Dad never quite made it, or Mom was more comfortable hiding behind an apron than letting the world see the paintings she hid in the attic.

Look at your spouse, your friend, your business associate. Does he look like a failure? Can you see the potential hidden beneath her traditions? Then help them dig for it, encourage them to exchange one tradition for another. Even Tevye realized that his traditions were new once.

> Love . . . it's a new style. On the other hand, our old ways were once new, weren't they? On the other hand, they decided [to be married] without parents, without a matchmaker. On the other hand, did Adam and Eve have a matchmaker? Yes, they did. Then it seems these two have the same matchmaker.[3]

The "new style" was a tremendous change from the way marriages were arranged in Anatevka. It also involved a tremendous personal change in the way Tevye saw his responsibility toward his children, himself, and God.

Yet, if change is good, especially in the fictitious village of Anatevka, then why is it so hard in real life?

Change

We asked six-year-old Anna to define the word *change.*

"Well," she said without hesitation, "it's when you tell me to take off one set of clothes and put on another."

For Anna, change was as simple as that. But the kind of change that takes place in therapy is not as simple as changing one pair of pants for another, or a used coffee filter for a new one.

The kind of change that occurs inside a person takes time. Ponder the words of Isaiah, "But they that wait upon the Lord shall renew their strength. They shall mount up with wings like eagles; they shall run and not be weary; they shall walk and not faint" (Isaiah 40:31).

Change in the way a person thinks about self, life, and God isn't accomplished in a few sessions. Some people expect a loved one to walk into a counselor's office and rattle off a couple of problems. They expect the therapist to utter a few magic words, throw out a couple of suggestions, and POOF! instant change, instant better life.

It will never happen. What does happen is an opportunity to look at all the dirty laundry spread out on the floor—an opportunity for self-examination.

This results more often in embarrassment, resentment, disbelief and horror, not in an instantly regenerated self-concept. And the deeper the pile on the floor, the longer the process.

In her book, *The Dance of Intimacy,* Dr. Harriet Lerner says:

> In our rapidly changing society we can count on only two things that will never change. What will never change is the will to change and the fear of change. It is the will to change that motivates us to seek help. It is the fear of change that motivates us to resist the very help we seek.[4]

Steps Toward Change

• LOOKING AT ONESELF DIFFERENTLY. Elizabeth came into therapy with faulty ideas about herself and many negative traditions. Although she had the will to change, she was also scared to death.

British philosopher Edmund Burke said, "No passion so effectually robs the mind of all its powers of action and reasoning as fear." Fear is very powerful and keeps many people from continuing the work of counseling.

My job as her therapist was to help Elizabeth at least

consider looking at herself differently. That was the first step toward change. The following are some of those faulty beliefs and traditions she needed to change.

Elizabeth was convinced she was a failure and destined to always be one. Every time she looked in a mirror, she saw an ugly face looking back at her. Like many victims of sexual abuse, Elizabeth had trouble enjoying her husband.

"Sex is awful," she said. "I can't even stand to let him touch me—it makes me sick to my stomach." The past harm that Elizabeth endured had ruined what God intended to be the most precious treasure a husband and wife can give each other.

Elizabeth had the temperament of a hornet at times, and the slightest upset would send her buzzing into a blind rage. Then when the rage left she would slip into a deep melancholy—just like Dad.

She saw herself as the world's worst mother. Even though David and the kids tried to assure her, Elizabeth was convinced she lacked any nurturing skills and would surely cause her children deep emotional wounds.

How could she think otherwise? Her own mother lacked the skills; so did her grandmother and, I suspect, her great-grandmother. This was tradition.

The pile of laundry Elizabeth and I had to sort through was obviously very deep. But not so deep she couldn't change.

"Why is she like this?" asked David. "Why won't she just control herself? It's so easy."

"It's *not* easy," I said. "Elizabeth has learned to behave certain ways in order to cope, to exist, even to stay alive. From Elizabeth's perspective, change is tantamount to treason."

"Treason?" said David. "I'm not asking her to desert her country or give away vital military secrets."

"Well," I smiled, "in a sense you are. We both are."

Ending one tradition in order to start something new is much like an act of desertion. Elizabeth felt this strongly. In a very real sense she was committing treason. In essence, she was telling her family of origin, "I don't believe in what you stand for. I refuse to buy into your way of life. I have found a better way to live and be happy." Elizabeth wanted to defect.

Whew! Who wants to tell their family those things? Surely they will fire back. Especially when they find out you *have* been giving away vital secrets. No one wants to engage in more battles or watch their family fall apart. In most cases when secrets are confronted and dealt with inside the family, they do not disintegrate, although some reshuffling of roles may take place.

Elizabeth had other fears. She worried that no one would like her if she changed. She feared alienating her family and friends. What if she discovered she married the wrong man, because she was not the same person she later discovered under the soot and grime?

These fears are real. Bad things *can* happen when we dare to change. It was Jesus who said:

> And who would patch an old garment with unshrunk cloth? For the patch would tear away and make the hole worse. And who would use old wineskins to store new wine? For the old skins would burst with the pressure, and the wine would be spilled and the skins ruined. Only new wineskins are used to store new wine. That way both are preserved (Matthew 9:16-17).

• OVERCOMING SURVIVAL GUILT. Elizabeth's deeply ambivalent feelings were not unusual. When people consider change or make changes in their lives, they often experience what we term "survival guilt." They find themselves trying to answer questions like, "Why me? Why am I the one to get better? Why not my sister or brother?"

This is not unlike the guilt felt by survivors of an airplane crash or fire. Even men and women who do not grow up in Christian homes and find the Lord later have a sense of "Why me?" They carry a feeling of leaving the others behind.

There were times in therapy when all of these fears converged and Elizabeth would visibly tremble. She was shaken to the very core of her being. Change was necessary. She knew it. I knew it. David knew it. The children knew it. But how do you get around such fear? The first step is facing it—head-on.

"I could not have done it without you," said Elizabeth. "I thought for sure the building would collapse around me when I finally spoke the truth. I thought my feelings were that powerful. But they weren't."

Sometimes feelings and fears can seem so strong that, like a tornado, they will destroy everything and everyone in their path. Therapy teaches patients that feelings are not that strong and powerful.

• PUTTING RESPONSIBILITY WHERE IT BELONGS. Elizabeth has finally been able to at least consider that she isn't quite as ugly as she thought. She's willing to try to think of herself not as a failure in *all* areas of life, but as someone with great potential and talent. "Well, *almost* all," she said. Now what?

Well, now comes the difficult task of putting the responsibility for her faulty ideas or lies where they belong. As we stated earlier, the purpose of looking at the past is not to place blame, but to find responsibility.

Blame is a damning word. Responsibility has more to do with finding the source and holding someone accountable. For Elizabeth, the source of her faulty self-image was her parents. Although she first had to deal with volcanoes of anger, and downpours of sadness toward them, she was able to eventually see them as human beings capable of mistakes—human beings with their own faulty self-images.

This step is a big change with many benefits. Up to this point Elizabeth's life was like a polluted creek. There was so much trash and filth floating around it was impossible to see the beauty way down deep where a garden of life was trying to grow.

Now that the junk had been cleaned away, Elizabeth was free to see herself more clearly, more accurately—not only herself but her family, friends, and God.

It should be emphasized that the purpose of therapy is not to eradicate the human condition and turn out perfect people. We won't be perfect until we see God. We live in a fallen, sinful world where there is no perfection. Life will always have problems, and even people who go through the waters of therapy will continue to struggle. We hope that they will have learned how to navigate around or through these struggles more effectively.

● APPLYING NEW TRUTHS TO LIFE. For some people this third step means confronting their abuser or source of their depression and anxiety. For others it is driving across a bridge—*alone*—and getting safely to the other side.

Sometimes it means standing up to convictions. In *Fiddler on the Roof,* Motel, who was very much in love with Tevye's oldest daughter, found the courage to stand up to Tevye. Tevye tells Motel, "You're just a poor tailor." Bravely, Motel pulls himself up and says, "That's true, Reb Tevye, but even a poor tailor is entitled to some happiness."[5]

Although David wanted Elizabeth to change, he had his own ambivalence to deal with. Change is often just as scary for the spouse or family or friends.

"Sure, I want her to change," said David. "At least change the things *I* think need changing."

But what about the things only Elizabeth wanted to

change? She and David both wanted to see an end to the fits of rage, and the gray, wintry depression that blanketed the whole family.

David looked forward to the day when he and his wife could meander the mall without Elizabeth having one of her "spells," his word for the strangling panic attacks and claustrophobia Elizabeth experienced.

"It's embarrassing," he said. "We run out of the mall like two pinballs in a machine. Then once we're outside, she starts breathing heavy, like she just ran a marathon. Now that kind of change I could handle." It wasn't that David wasn't compassionate. He was just tired.

David had some minor fears about how Elizabeth would "turn out," as he put it. But for the most part he was happy with her progress. He still wondered if she would *ever* get all the socks in the house organized, but at least she didn't cry over them anymore.

For some couples, change can be more difficult. I had a case where a man was entrenched in taking care of his wife. The fear of her becoming independent rattled him so much he would do things to sabotage the progress she was making. Wives who have become accustomed to handling the household—everything from discipline to bills to even mowing the lawn fear the new assertiveness and confidence their husbands display.

"I'm afraid he'll take over completely," said one wife. "Then I won't be important."

The good news is that the therapist's office does not resemble Dr. Frankenstein's laboratory. The doctor or counselor is not creating an entirely new person. People leave therapy basically the way they went in—just better. Their previously frozen personality traits have been thawed, and they are more confident and expressive and enjoyable.

In cases where fears can be damaging or paralyzing to

relationships, some form of couples counseling can help. Generally it is short-term, and couples easily discover ways to balance and support each other.

Making the Exchange

David and Elizabeth pulled into the mall parking lot. As usual David cruised around looking for the perfect spot to park.

As he pushed the gearshift into park and released his safety belt, he noticed Elizabeth had turned suddenly quiet. She was preoccupied, staring blankly through the windshield.

"Hey," said David, "the Eagle has landed. We can get out now."

Elizabeth turned suddenly. "I'm sorry," she said, clutching the brown bag containing the too-large sweater that needed to be returned.

"I've been thinking," she continued. "Maybe you should let me return the sweater myself, just me."

David chuckled. "You?" he said. "You've never been able to return anything. You're scared of salespeople, remember? You're afraid you'll get yelled at."

"I know," said Elizabeth. "That was the old me. I think I can do it now."

"Okay," smiled David. "This I've got to see. I'll stay reasonably close in case you get the bends or something."

Together they laughed as they made their way to the store. Elizabeth stopped a moment at the door. Her heart started to pound and beads of perspiration popped out on her forehead.

"I knew it," said David. "Give me the bag."

"No," said Elizabeth. "I am going to do this."

She managed her way through the labyrinth of racks and people to the sweater department. She stared at the woman behind the counter. At first Elizabeth thought she saw hair on the woman's knuckles and fangs in her mouth, but she didn't let that stop her. This time she was going all the way.

Elizabeth approached the counter. "Can I help you?" asked the woman. Elizabeth swallowed hard. "I need to return this sweater. It's . . . it's not that there's anything wrong or it's ugly or something. It doesn't fit. I've lost some weight. It kind of droops on me like a sack."

The woman smiled and pulled the sweater and sales slip from the bag and made the simple return.

Elizabeth turned on her heel. She shot David a quick smile and stuffed the $47.99 into her pocket. Elizabeth had just become richer—in many ways.

This may seem like a trivial incident, but it was important. For the first time in many years Elizabeth asserted herself. She confronted her fear of having a panic attack every time she entered a store. She talked with a stranger and told her exactly what she needed. And she got it. No questions asked.

Shortly after Elizabeth's triumph, she and David were cruising the mall when she spotted a pay phone. "Wait," she said. "I need to make a call." David couldn't imagine who Elizabeth had to call.

From the sound of her voice on the other end of the phone line, I knew Elizabeth had just experienced a small yet important victory.

Chapter Eight
Staying Close by Keeping Your Distance

"Mama, Mama," sang Anna, skipping into her parents' bedroom. "Is it time now? Will you help me with my new puzzle? It's very hard—200 pieces."

Elizabeth continued sorting socks. *I hate socks,* she thought. *No matter what I do, the same number that goes in the dryer does not come out.*

"Mama," shouted Anna. "Help me!"

"Help what?" asked Elizabeth. "Are you okay?"

Anna pursed her lips and twisted her arms around her chest. "Mama," she said, "I want you to help me with my puzzle. You promised yesterday. You promised we would spend time together today—just us. You crossed your heart and everything."

Elizabeth swallowed hard and took a deep breath. "Not today, Anna. Mama's tired and I have all this stuff to do before Daddy gets home."

"Can I help?" asked Anna.

"No," answered Elizabeth. "Just run along. Find someone else to play with."

"But Mama," said Anna, "I don't want to play with someone else. I want you."

Elizabeth could see the tears in Anna's eyes, and she hated to disappoint her so much. But she just didn't have the energy.

"Anna," said Elizabeth, "sit up here on the bed with me. We'll talk, you know, girl to girl."

Anna climbed next to her mom and sat cross-legged.

"I guess we haven't been spending much time together," said Elizabeth. "It's not because I don't want to. I think about us doing lots of things together—the museum, the mall, lots of stuff."

"We don't have to go to the museum," said Anna. "Just put the puzzle together."

"Anna, I'm trying to explain that I just can't be with you a lot right now."

"Yeah, I know," pouted Anna. "Daddy says you're depressed. He said you're not much good for anything right now."

"Well, he shouldn't have put it like that. But yes, I'm depressed. It's a disease, only you can't see it. You don't get a fever and you almost never throw up. But I'm still sick. And you know when you're really sick how tired you feel. You don't want to play with anybody."

"When will you get better, Mama?"

"I don't know. Might be a while yet. But I'm taking my medicine and seeing the doctor regularly. I think I'm getting better. Won't Dad be thrilled when he sees what I've done with the socks?"

Anna looked at the mountain of unmatched socks on the bed. "Well, I guess the pile is smaller." She giggled.

"I know I break a lot of promises," continued Elizabeth. "I'm really sorry."

Anna threw her arms around Elizabeth and squeezed hard. "I love you," she whispered.

Elizabeth felt her own tears sting her face. She wanted to tell Anna how much she loved her. But the words got stuck, like something too sweet in her throat.

Intimacy

It's possible that the puzzle was not the most important thing on Anna's mind. It was likely a vehicle she chose to get her mama's attention. What she really wanted was to be close to Elizabeth—to be intimate.

Intimacy is not a word to be used only when describing sexual closeness. There are many ways people need intimacy in their lives.

Intimacy is a close, private experience between individuals (usually two) that is not necessarily shared with anyone else. Not only are these times close, but they are also closed—closed from outward or inward distraction. These are times when two people focus only on each other and the object or feeling that has brought them together.

Perhaps they didn't realize it, but the little talk that Elizabeth and Anna just had was very intimate. It didn't last long. It didn't need to. Good things do come in small packages.

Intimacy, like anything else worth having, takes time. True intimacy is reserved for long-term relationships. As Dr. Lerner points out, "It is only in long-term relationships that we are called upon to navigate that delicate balance between separateness and connectedness and that we confront the challenge of sustaining both—without losing either when the going gets tough."[1]

When someone we love is going through therapy, there will undoubtedly be times when intimacy and togetherness will need to be placed on the back burner for a while.

This is to be expected even though it is not pleasant. As we've seen already, the process of therapy or counseling requires a tremendous amount of energy.

Self-exploration, exposing past wounds, feeling the feelings that have been stuffed inside, breaking some of the rules we've learned growing up, daring to see ourselves differently, refusing to believe the lies learned in childhood—all this makes a body, spirit, and mind *tired!*

Not only is the person weighed down by the physical effects of depression and anxiety, but the actual therapy process is exhausting. Often a patient or client is left with little energy reserve—perhaps just enough to get through some daily chores. This is one reason intimacy gets sidelined.

"At first I didn't know what to expect," remembers Elizabeth. "I knew there would be a lot of talk about my childhood, but I had no idea how exhausting it would be. Sometimes I would leave a session feeling like I had just been hit by a train."

Elizabeth's complaint echoes the voices of many. Therapy is exhausting. Not only that, but it becomes a preoccupation as a client tries to sort out all the stuff she's been discussing with her doctor or counselor.

"What I didn't like were all the dark, silent times," said David. "She was on another planet as far as I was concerned. Sometimes it made me angry, because I thought she was neglecting me and the kids."

Elizabeth didn't like those times either. "We were so far apart," she says. "Maybe I was on another planet, in a way. Knowing David and the kids were troubled by my space travel made me feel guilty."

"So here I was smothering in guilt and depression," she

continued. "I felt guilty because I was discussing my parents with the doctor, guilty because of the feelings that kept erupting all over the place, and guilty because it touched the family."

How could anyone be intimate with all that going on? Intimacy involves the ability to fully give oneself to another, to be involved physically, emotionally, and spiritually. When a person's sense of *self* has never really developed, or somewhere along the line has gotten all scrambled around, it's pretty hard to want to share it with someone else.

To quote Dr. Lerner again, "We move up on the selfhood scale (and intimacy scale) when we are able to:

– Present a balanced picture of both our strengths and our vulnerabilities.

– Make clear statements of our beliefs, values, and priorities, and then keep our behavior congruent with these.

– Stay emotionally connected to significant others, even when things get pretty intense.

– Address difficult and painful issues and take a position on matters important to us.

– State our differences and allow others to do the same.[2]

The Hatching Stage

While it may be necessary to take a time-out from intimacy, remember that this too will pass. Although Elizabeth wasn't able to enjoy the intimate feelings she once experienced with David or the kids, she was not sitting idle. Part of therapy involves learning to be intimate with yourself.

That means getting comfortable with yourself and your feelings, accepting your own humanity—warts and all. This allows the freedom and vulnerability necessary to be intimate with someone else.

Therapy for the loved one on the other side of the couch involves a lot of waiting. Part of that process is waiting for intimacy to bloom or return in your relationship.

It can be a difficult time for a loved one. So much is hidden from view. This desert time is what one psychologist called the Hatching Stage of development. She likened it to watching and waiting for an egg to hatch. You know there are all kinds of wonderful things going on inside that shell. Eventually it cracks and out comes a small, wet baby chicken.

Disturbing the egg while it is hatching can cause irreparable harm. But what emerges from the egg still needs gentle care to further develop. "'Tis hard. But what may not be altered is made lighter by patience" (Horace).

Waiting is never easy. Even the Prophet Habakkuk had trouble waiting. He wriggled and squirmed like anyone hoping for an answer. But God is sovereign and His timing is perfect. As He told Habakkuk:

> But these things I plan won't happen right away. Slowly, steadily, surely, the time approaches when the vision will be fulfilled. If it seems slow, do not despair, for these things will surely come to pass. Just be patient! They will not be overdue a single day! (Habakkuk 2:3)

Hide these words in your heart as you wait for your friend to come home to you and fully be with you.

God created people to have relationships. We are physically, emotionally, and spiritually designed to have relationships. God would not allow your wife, husband, child, or friend to be repackaged by a counselor in such a way that he or she no longer needs you or wants you.

Instead your spouse or friend will hopefully become a person more equipped to have a deeper relationship with you, a higher level of intimacy, a more comfortable togetherness.

Oh, What a Ministry!

The Bible has much to say about the Christian's role as minister. Not just professional clergy, but lay people engaged in ministry to people on the street, business associates, children, friends, and spouses. About this last group Larry Crabb puts it beautifully:

> To be able to profoundly influence another human being in a way that promotes a fulfilling awareness of their wholeness in Christ is a thrilling opportunity. A sovereign God has selected me from among the billions of men whoever lived for a ministry to which He has called no one else: the ministry of loving my wife with the unique committed love of a husband. How sad to think of the responsibilities of husband or wife as mere obligation or duty.[3]

It took time, but David was able to see this time-out with his wife as another part of his ministry as the one and only husband for her. He worked hard not to pressure her for closeness, although he sometimes failed. He realized she was going through the very deepest waters of therapy and the best he could do for her was to wait.

This is not to say that waiting is easy. No one likes to wait. Standing in line at the grocery store is enough to make us want to scream. Waiting for a wife or husband or friend to "hatch" is infinitely more difficult.

It will happen. Take comfort in the fact that you are not alone in this desert. Even Paul had Apollos. "I planted," said Paul. "Apollos watered. But it was God who caused the garden to grow in their hearts."

David had me. As Elizabeth's doctor I planted seeds of

change. David helped them along by continuing to love, nurture, and minister to Elizabeth. But it is certainly God who causes the desert to blossom.

During these times when you can't seem to tune your wife or husband into the intimacy channel, it is natural to get frustrated. But try not to let your frustration get the best of you. Do not force your spouse into doing anything he or she is not emotionally prepared to do.

Any kind of unasked for sexual play could be construed as abuse all over again. Don't panic. Just back away and allow your spouse to take the initiative. Even if all he or she can handle is a little snuggling, see it as a step toward greater intimacy.

When you do engage in sexual activity, go slowly. You may need to be prepared to stop at any point and revert to some other form of loving but nonsexual closeness.

Don't take your spouse's refusals personally. It is not about you. It is the childhood abuser or rapist your spouse is refusing. And that's good.

This may be the time to emphasize other forms of intimacy . . . simply sharing a walk together, watching the sunset or sunrise. Even watching television together can help fill the void.

If your spouse is unable to have a social life, accept it, but continue to visit friends, go to church and Bible study. Sooner or later your spouse will probably ask to go along.

Family Intimacy

We said earlier that intimacy is usually between two people. Yet, families need some shared "we" times as well. Mealtimes can be good opportunities for this. The important point is being together in one place, doing the same thing, having the same goal.

"I don't know if you call this intimacy," said Elizabeth, "but I'm afraid of tunnels. I get very claustrophobic. So whenever we go on a trip and we come to a tunnel that we can't bypass without losing hours off our travel time, David and the kids help me through it. As we're passing through this deep, dark tunnel they sing. They sing as loud as they can—usually theme songs from television programs. It gets me through. It feels nice. We all have the same focus, the same desire—get Mama through the tunnel."

What do you think? Sound like togetherness, closeness, sharing a common idea? Intimacy can wear many faces.

Friendship

Most of this chapter has focused on spouses and families. Friendships can also be very intimate. Friends suffer similar losses when someone they deeply care about is distant.

"I love Millicent. She's my best friend. We've been together since high school. She's always been there for me, and I've been there for her. But when therapy gets treacherous and exhausting, or I get so preoccupied with things, it's hard to be with her. Mostly, I think it's because I don't have anything to say. I'm boring."

Elizabeth's friend needed to accept this time of separateness. For a while Elizabeth couldn't even talk to her on the phone. She was blessed because Millicent was a true friend. She stayed close enough to know when she was needed, and far away enough to make Elizabeth comfortable.

This is the stuff of friendship—caring enough to know how close to stand, understanding enough to know when to be close.

Chapter Nine
What Do I Tell the Kids?

What follows is a paraphrase of a familiar portion of Scripture. We believe it best explains the family system and the importance of each member of the household.

> The family has many members, not just one. If the father says, "I am not a member of the family because I am not a mother," that does not make him any less a part of the family. And what would you think if you heard a mother say, "I am not part of the family because I am only a mother, not a father"? If a child says, "I am not part of the family because I am not a mother or a father," that does not make the child any

> less a member of the family. Suppose the whole family were a father—then who would cook the meals? Or if the whole family were a mother, who would mow the lawn?
>
> But that isn't the way God has made us. He has made many members for the family and has put each member just where he wants them. What a strange thing a family would be if it had only one member! So he has made many members, but still there is only one family.
>
> The father can never say to the mother, "I don't need you." The mother can't say to the children, "I don't need you."
>
> And some of the members who seem weakest and least important are really important. Yes, we should be especially glad to have some members who seem rather small! So God has put the family together in such a way that extra honor and care are given to those members who might otherwise seem less important. This makes for happiness among the members, so that the members have the same care for each other as they do for themselves. If one member suffers, all members suffer as well, and if one member is honored, all the members are glad (1 Corinthians 12:14-26, authors' paraphrase).

A family is a system designed by God and made up of individual members. Each individual is as important as the others and should be esteemed as such.

The family exists for the growth of every member. When this purpose is forgotten or violated by incest, abuse, alcoholism, or other crises, the family no longer benefits the individual. The individual now exists to keep the family from a feared collapse.

It has only been in recent years that professionals have

seen the importance of taking children out of a subcategory of nonpersonhood and esteeming them in importance with the adult members of the family.

No longer does the axiom, "Children should be seen and not heard," rule the roost. It was once thought that truly caring parents would do anything to protect a child from stresses they considered too difficult for the child.

We have since learned that although they should not be treated as adults, children can handle much of what life dishes out. This does not mean that they are to be left alone to assimilate crises and understand the ills of life alone. They still need the special protection of their parents.

"I Don't Want to Be Like You!"

"Oh, great," shouted Daniel. "I guess this means I can't have Ben over for Nintendo—*again!*"

Elizabeth blew her nose and dabbed her teary eyes. "I'm sorry," she said. "I'm just having a bad day."

"Every day is a bad day, and I think it stinks. I want out of this stupid family. It's not fair."

"Danny, listen," said Elizabeth, moving toward him. "I said I was sorry. I know how hard this is for you. I *will* get better."

Daniel shook his head. "No, you won't," he hollered. "Just like Dad said, we all have a thorn in the flesh, and you're ours."

Elizabeth tried to stop a gush of tears. "Daniel," she snapped, "you don't know what you're saying. I'm sure your father had something different in mind when he said that."

"I do so know what I'm saying. This stinks!" Daniel was silent as he stared at his mother's red face. "I just don't know what you're crying about."

"So you feel scared or left out?"

"Yeah," said Daniel. "I don't know what is happening. Dad told me it's like you have a disease."

"Depression," said Elizabeth.

"Well, what if I get it? I don't want to be like you!"

That was what was really troubling thirteen-year old Daniel. He was afraid of his mother's disease—afraid of what it was doing to her, and afraid that it might happen to him.

As any parent of a teenager knows, these are the roller coaster years. It is during this time that children really begin to grab hold of their own identity. Much of a child's perception of himself comes from the way the family interacts and relates to each other. He sees himself reflected back to him from his parents.

Daniel had just turned nine when Elizabeth started therapy. It wasn't until he turned eleven that he really started to notice Elizabeth's behavior. He had heard the crying and the arguing, and he felt sad when Elizabeth couldn't be available to him—physically, emotionally, or spiritually. He was not unaffected by his mother's illness.

Daniel had also experienced times of tension within himself. Like many children he feared that somehow he had caused his mother's illness. He often felt insecure and acted out his feelings of helplessness with tantrums and insults.

But this last year had been particularly tough. Now, he saw how his own life was being affected by Elizabeth's depression and anxieties. He started asking questions and felt concern for the future of his family.

"So many kids' parents are getting divorced," he said, "over stupider things than you guys argue about. We're learning about depression and stuff in school. A lot of depressed people kill themselves. I remember you and Dad talking about it—a long time ago—but I remember."

Daniel remembered correctly. Children have a way of

hearing and remembering even the most secretive bathroom conversations. Sometimes parents will have no idea that their child has overheard a conversation until months or even years later.

Children love to listen to adults talk. They learn so much, not just from what we say, but how we say it. They tune into our moods, simply by watching us move and observing our facial expressions. They are very sensitive to emotion—verbal and nonverbal expression. Children are like sponges, absorbing everything in their path.

At the time of Elizabeth's suicide threat, Daniel was eleven. Because of their fear of the subject and Elizabeth's high emotional state, nothing was said at the time. David and Elizabeth also believed Daniel wasn't old enough to understand something as gut-wrenching as suicide. But obviously Daniel heard something, and he hung onto it until just the right time to repeat it.

Like many thoughtful parents, Elizabeth and David wanted to hide this experience from him—for his own protection. Given Daniel's age at the time, this was a good decision.

But now the time had come for Daniel to be welcomed into Elizabeth and David's adult world, at least one giant step inside. By the time a child turns thirteen, he or she is a young adult. But remember, the emphasis is on *young.* Daniel still had one foot in the toy box.

It was not appropriate for Daniel to be told everything that was going on with Mom or between Mom and Dad. Some things should remain private. But at his age and level of maturity, Elizabeth and David knew he could handle many facts about Elizabeth's condition that Anna could not. They were careful not to lead or bait Daniel. Generally, they waited until he brought up a particular subject, and then they were careful to give him only the most important information—just enough to answer the question.

In this way Daniel felt special and necessary. But he didn't become a therapist for Elizabeth. Some parents tend to place their children in the difficult position of confidant. It wasn't Daniel's place to sort out his mother's struggles or know every detail of her life.

Because of the honesty with which his parents shared Elizabeth's recovery process, Daniel was able to support and encourage his mom—from a young adult perspective.

Through his parents' honesty and willingness to discuss their problems, Daniel learned skills that will help him deal with other problems and conflicts all through his life.

By watching the example of his parents, Daniel learned to allow himself to have feelings, good and bad. He knew he could discuss those feelings within the family and voice his own opinions, whether or not the rest of the family agreed. This also provided an arena for Daniel to bring out his intuitions. Even though he wasn't certain about some things, he felt the freedom to lay them on the table.

It also gave David and Elizabeth an opportunity to correct any faulty impressions Daniel was having. At one point he was convinced his parents would be divorcing. He held his fear inside for a long time, and then it just popped out.

"I know what's going on," he said one day. "You guys are splitting up."

David and Elizabeth were shocked by Daniel's revelation. Nothing could have been further from the truth.

"No, we are not," said David. "Where did you get that idea?"

"Well, for one thing, you guys don't always sleep together—like husbands and wives are supposed to. And you have been doing a lot of fighting. Or else Mom is always sad or angry. The other day she even yelled at the mailman. Ben says that's just how his folks acted before the Big D word hit."

Elizabeth took Daniel by the arm. "We need to talk,"

she said. "There's a different reason Dad and I don't sleep together most nights."

"Like what?" Daniel smirked.

David sat next to Elizabeth and placed his arm around her shoulder. "Do you want me to tell him?"

"No, I'm all right," she said.

Elizabeth took Daniel's hand. He felt uncomfortable at first and tried to wriggle away, but Elizabeth held on tightly.

"Now listen," she said. "This won't be easy to say and it won't be easy to hear. When I was nine years old up until I was twelve, your Uncle Richard . . . well, he . . . he raped me."

Elizabeth couldn't hold back tears. It is a memory she will always remember with sadness.

Daniel squeezed his mother's hand. "O Mom," he said. "Just like the kids on the news?"

Elizabeth nodded.

"That's right, Dan," said David. "That is what Mom is really angry about. And it's that very bad memory that makes it hard for her to sleep with me some nights."

Daniel had many questions. So Elizabeth and David sat with him, answering each one as openly and lovingly as they could. Daniel learned a horrible truth that evening, but he also saw how much his parents loved each other . . . a love he now knew would endure anything if it could endure that kind of pain.

Although the crisis of Elizabeth's depression was not a pleasant experience for any of them, it did allow a stage to be built on which family members could play out their feelings and reactions to her illness.

Our intention is not to paint an overly rosy picture of how this family handled their problems. There were many difficult times of uncertainty and distrust, times when thoughts of divorce did creep into David's and Elizabeth's minds.

But with careful guidance and the willingness of both Elizabeth and David to share their family struggles with me and trusted church friends, they were able to head off major family problems.

What about Anna?

Someone once said that a house isn't a home until it's been touched with love. Well, a mother isn't a mom until she can feel good about herself.

"I remember walking into this antique store," said Elizabeth. "I was eight and one-half months pregnant with Anna. It was blazing hot. I got out of the car and thought for certain I had just stepped on molten lava. So I ducked into this little store for some relief. And there, hanging above the door was an old, rickety sign that read, 'If Mama ain't happy, ain't nobody happy!'

"That is so true. I never realized how my moods and feelings and behavior affected the whole family, even stuff I tried to hide."

For many reasons, Anna was more stressed by her mother's therapy and mood problems than Daniel. Anna was only three when Elizabeth came to see me. Prior to actually beginning therapy, Elizabeth was struggling with emotional symptoms that made it hard for her to truly bond or connect with Anna.

"I knew something was wrong. I didn't have the same feelings about Anna as I did for Dan, but I couldn't understand it. I thought I must be the worst mother in the world."

Sadly, Anna and Elizabeth did not have a good beginning. But in time, after working on lots and lots of issues about her own mother, and with love and nurture, Elizabeth was able to slowly connect with Anna.

Anna felt her mother's sadness deeply. She knew when Elizabeth was angry. She grew resentful of any time Elizabeth and I spent on the phone. Without exception, she knew when I called, and she would do everything in her power to get Elizabeth to hang up. Although she could not express it, Anna was jealous of me. She thought I was taking her mama away. Anna felt abandoned each time I called or every time Elizabeth left the house for an appointment.

In the beginning Elizabeth was so preoccupied that she didn't think to reassure Anna when she left. No matter how young a child is, you need to make sure they are told when you will be back.

Three-year olds cannot be talked to like older children. They don't have the thinking skills or emotional capacity to understand that Mommy is depressed. They are not able to absorb and assimilate the feelings expressed by the people around them. They are very egocentric and believe that everything happens because of them.

But a depressed parent, spouse, other family member, or close friend can still talk with a preschool child. Many of the same principles we used in our illustration with Daniel apply to Anna.

"Sometimes it was enough just to say, 'Mommy is sad,' or, 'Mommy needs a hug,' " said Elizabeth. Sometimes all you can do is reassure a child with lots of hugs and kisses. Other times you just have to muster up the strength to read a story. A lot can happen in a short connection.

It is important that spouses or other family members keep the child's daily routine as uninterrupted as possible. Mom may have to take over in areas Dad used to handle, or maybe Dad will have to sew the nose back on a teddy bear.

Don't worry if you see a child this young doing some strange things. Three-year-olds have many tension outlets, including blinking, nail-biting, nose-picking, facial tics, and masturbation. Sometimes preschool children will regress when tension is high. Your newly potty-trained child may need diapers or training pants for a while. It's okay. These symptoms will go away.

As Anna grew older, Elizabeth was able to share more with her about what she was doing in therapy. In this way Anna was able to reevaluate what she was experiencing and, in a sense, have a new and improved experience.

She learned to give Elizabeth more space. Telephone calls got easier; not great, but easier. Anna and Elizabeth grew closer. Elizabeth was sure to answer any questions as fully as needed for Anna to be satisfied.

Younger children tend to need to talk about things over and over again. Be patient. No matter how often a subject comes up, talk about it. This is how a child discovers that it is okay to talk about feelings and things they don't understand.

By the time Anna was six, she and Elizabeth had built a pretty sound relationship. Anna still asked a lot of questions. She was moody and had a hard time not blaming herself for her mother's problems, but they talked about it.

In the same fashion that Daniel learned to assert himself and his needs, Anna developed the same skills.

"Mama, are you better or are you still sad?" asked Anna.

Elizabeth put her dish towel down and stooped to see Anna's eyes. "Well," she said, "I'm getting better. And I'm not as sad as before."

"Before what? Before me?"

"Oh, no," said Elizabeth. "My sadness has nothing to do with you. I feel sad for a lot of reasons that have nothing to do with you or Daniel or Daddy. I feel sad over things that happened when I was a kid."

Anna thought for a moment. "Then can we put a puzzle together?"

"Okay," said Elizabeth. "But only one. Remember how we talked before about how tired Mama gets right now?"

"I do," said Anna.

"The hardest times were when I lost my temper," said Elizabeth. "I would feel so awful looking into Anna's tear-streaked face. She just sobbed. Generally I screamed or hit her for really stupid reasons. When I saw her curl up on her bed and tuck her chin behind her knees, I remembered doing the same thing after my father hit me. Anna was just as defenseless and vulnerable as I was. I would stand there looking at her and feeling her pain; I felt my own pain and I also felt the pain of the sad little girl I still carry around inside my heart. I always apologized to Anna—always. I tried to explain as best I could why I acted the way I did. I told her she didn't deserve that treatment. I knew it wouldn't completely take away the hurt. I just prayed that it would soften it—even a little."

Elizabeth was doing all she could to make a bad situation better. She recognized her mistakes and admitted them, she wiped away the tears and talked with Anna.

"I felt so hopeless at those times," said David. "I would come home from work and I knew, I just knew that something had happened. I felt guilty because I didn't get home fifteen minutes sooner. I tried to comfort Anna and not get furious with Elizabeth. Some days I didn't even want to come home because I was afraid of the mess I would find. I thank God that Elizabeth never did any real damage to the kids. But still, the fear lingered for a long time."

Some General Guidelines for Parents

1. Keep lines of communication open. Welcome and answer any and all questions with age-appropriate responses.

2. Do not assume your children are oblivious to emotional undercurrents. Remember, part of communication is nonverbal, so watch your body language. Children pick up on everything. It has been said that children are the world's best tape recorders and the world's worst interpreters.

3. Do not insist there is nothing wrong. This will cause children to doubt their intuitions, not to talk about problems, and block uncomfortable thoughts in their own minds.
4. Children tend to always blame themselves for the family's problems. Reassure them constantly.
5. If you struggle with PMS, tell them, as long as they are at an age when they can understand. They will not hold it against you. They will more than likely want to comfort you.
6. Watch what gets blurted out in anger. Children believe everything they hear.
7. Acknowledge an argument. Don't brush it under the rug. Instead, talk with your kids about the fight. Ask them how they feel about it. Provide age-appropriate explanations for your behavior and for the argument.

Emphasize that your anger had nothing to do with them. Some older children can understand the phenomenon of transference if it is explained with words they understand.

If you feel you must leave the house for a while to cool down, tell the kids. But always tell them you will be back.

Apologize to children for arguing and show them that the disagreement has been resolved.

"I Love You, Mommy"

Children have a tremendous capacity to give and receive love. They are always ready with plenty of hugs and kisses, no matter how tough life gets. Even the most abused children will continue to love their parents. For in love there is hope and healing.

Children believe in the power of love in ways that adults have forgotten. When they are injured, they run to Mama or Daddy because they know it is their love that will take the pain away.

"I honestly don't know if I would have stuck with therapy if it wasn't for my kids," said Elizabeth. "Even when I thought I was failing, or therapy wasn't working, one of the kids would sense it and do something wonderful to keep me going. They were my best cheerleaders."

Anna was especially creative at giving her mom love when she least expected it.

"Anna was so cute," she said. "When she started to read and write, she found a whole new way to communicate. She loved to practice her letters a lot. I would find the ABCs scrawled on pieces of paper all over the house. Now she leaves me notes and drawings that say, 'I love you, Mama,' or 'Thanks for helping me do my homework.' Anna uses notes to ask for favors. I guess if she's not sure of my mood or how I'll answer, it's safer to ask in a note."

Daniel wasn't so open and obvious. "Daniel showed his love and support by taking out the trash without being asked. Or he would suddenly drop his Nintendo controller and set the table for dinner."

Children love to say "I Love You" in a variety of ways. Sometimes parents can get caught up in always being on the giving end of love. Given the chance, children are eager givers. If times are tough, don't hide it from your children. Let them know your feelings, and then let *them* hug and kiss *your* pain away.

Spouses of patients can find the same support in their children. Hugs work wonders. Even planning special get-away times for you and your kids can be uplifting. There are many ways to include children in the recovery process. By doing so you affirm their importance in the family. Most kids really *do* want to help.

Nearly 2,000 years ago a Roman writer said, "We owe the greatest respect to a child." We would do well to heed his ancient yet timely words.

Chapter Ten
Every Home Needs Supports

"Don't forget, I'm going over to church tonight," said David.

"Oh, that's right," said Elizabeth. "The support group. Are you sure you want to go?"

"Well, it sounds like it might help. Your doctor thought it would be a good idea."

"Yeah, but, well, I'm not so sure."

"Why not?" asked David. "All along you've been wanting me to be more supportive, to learn more about your problems. Now all of a sudden you don't want me to go."

"I guess I'm scared. I don't know how I feel about you discussing my problems with a bunch of other guys."

"Elizabeth," said David with frustration, "you talk to the

doctor about everything. Don't you think I need someone to talk things over with? This hasn't been easy, you know."

"Well, I just don't want my business blabbed all over church."

"I doubt that will happen. Something tells me there's a pretty strict code of honor in this group. I suspect every husband has been duly warned. Don't worry. And besides, if I think it will be like that, I'll leave. Trust me."

Support Groups

Over the past several years there has been growth of support groups. If you can name it, there is probably a support group for it. Some of the ones we have found are for weight control problems, allergies, shyness, adult children of alcoholics, adult children of dysfunctional families, stop-smoking groups, drug recovery groups, divorce groups, single parenting, and parenting support groups. The list could go on and on.

A support group differs from therapy or group therapy. The single most important aspect of the support group is that it does *not* exist to do therapy. The purpose of discussing problems and struggles is not to find causes or roots, but to offer support and encouragement to each member.

Support groups, particularly those with a Christian backing, are a visual example of Paul's admonishment to the Galatians. "Share each other's troubles and problems, and so obey our Lord's command" (Galatians 6:2).

The individual members find support in a variety of ways. The groups offer encouragement and give members opportunity to air frustrations; members listen to one another and learn ways to cope with specific problems.

Finding your way into a support group lessens your feelings of aloneness and offers an opportunity to fill some gaps in your need for intimacy and togetherness.

Support groups differ from group therapy in other ways. Group therapy is more businesslike with strictly defined rules, one of which is that members do not socialize outside the group. Doing so would tend to dilute the therapy process. All conversations must be within the group. Taking conversation outside means it will probably be left outside.

Group therapy sessions are run by professional counselors with experience and expertise in the type of emotional problems common to the group.

In a support group a person might ask another member, "Are you trying to rescue your wife?" But in a therapy session the question would be, "Why are you trying to rescue your wife?" The role of the support group is not to fix a person's faulty mind-set but to encourage each other to become comfortable in their loved one's world.

Support groups, although sometimes led by professionals, are more often conducted by laypersons with some training and experience. The best support groups are run by people who have had specific education and are able to keep the group on target, not allowing it to turn into a "bleeding heart" or "bashing" session.

Also, a person with some psychological training and awareness will be able to recognize those members of the group who may have a greater need, and can encourage them to seek other professional help.

Socialization is encouraged and friendships are often formed in support groups. In this way, what was begun in the group setting can continue. Most support groups meet for six to eight weeks. Because of this short time span, the members are asked to make a firm commitment to attend each meeting in order to keep continuity and build relationships.

Confidentiality is also integral to the support group. Just as in therapy or counseling, members need to be able to trust their leader as well as the other members of the group.

Elizabeth was afraid that her business would be blabbed all over church if David attended a support group. That fear should be dispelled immediately. The group is where spouses, friends, or family members will come to understand their loved one's need for privacy, as they freely discuss, possibly for the first time, their own deep and scary feelings.

"You Too?"

David, Elizabeth, and their children attended a large suburban church that offered support groups for divorce recovery and unemployment, as well as a newly established one for prosurvivors of sexual abuse.

This group was for people who loved someone with a history of sexual trauma, whether it was childhood incest, rape, or other abuse. David's group was all male, each man was married to a woman who had been sexually molested.

The only woman in the group was the leader. She had been sexually abused, went through the waters of therapy, and came out the other side healed and whole and able to give support to those who were hurting.

Like most first-time participants David hung around outside the meeting room, spying out the land, as it were, as the other men slowly found their way into the room. He was just about to walk through the door when he felt a hand on his shoulder.

David turned quickly. "You too?" said Paul. David and Paul had served as church ushers together. They attended the same Sunday School class and even did their time as guardians of the nursery together. But over all the years of their friendship, they never knew the secret they shared—until now.

David felt his heart beat fast, and he wiped his sweaty palms against his pant legs.

"Paul," he asked, "why are you here? Not Sarah?"

Paul took a deep breath. "Yes," he said. "Sarah. I've known for a while. We managed to keep her illness quiet but now it's, well, just too much. She's been a total wreck and the kids are all upset. What should I do? She keeps going off her medication. At first I wanted to. . . . "

Just then the group leader approached. "It would be a really good idea if you guys would continue this conversation inside, with the rest of the group."

David and Paul looked at each other and then took their place in the group. They were fortunate. They knew each other and so some of the initial nervousness and embarrassment that comes with attending a group like this was lessened.

After introductions and a short prayer time, the leader set out the goals and rules. Then the group started. Paul was able to finish telling David, and the group, how his first reaction was to "kill my father-in-law."

Other group members agreed and voiced their own sometimes violent reactions to their wives' disclosures.

Most of the men spoke about their struggles, but some remained silent. This can happen in support groups. Eventually people will speak, but it takes time to build trust and to get over a kind of stage fright that goes with group territory.

By the fourth meeting David had heard many horror stories and learned about other emotional problems that can stem from sexual trauma. Particularly Sarah's. She was diagnosed as manic-depressive.

Although manic-depression is also manifested in people who have not been sexually abused, it is often seen in those women who have experienced some form of sexual degradation.

Manic-depression or bipolar depression is an illness that manifests itself with alternating bouts of "highs" or mania and "lows" or depression. It is a difficult illness to treat and a frustrating one to live with.

"I can't stand it," said Paul, at one of the meetings. "She stops taking her medication and goes completely wild. She spends all our money on . . . on junk and runs up the credit cards."

Paul went on to complain about how his wife gets "revved up" during the manic phase of her illness and goes for "days without sleep." He also told about times when she had almost killed herself by driving too fast. He even told the group about the speeding tickets—"enough to paper the bathroom."

For Paul, and many other people living with someone with manic-depression, a lot of time is spent on damage control—returning unnecessary purchases, calling creditors, making certain the patient is never alone, and sometimes even arranging for hospitalization.

Hospitalization

"I hate doing this," said Paul. "It feels almost criminal. But I know it's the only way."

"I don't know if I could ever commit Elizabeth," said David.

Paul sighed. "If it was the only way to save her life, your marriage, and sanity, you would."

Paul told the group that Sarah had been in the hospital three other times that year. "It's usually only for a week or two. Then she's all right—as long as she takes her medication. I encourage her as much as I can, but she's the one who has to swallow the pills."

David could hear both the sadness and anger in Paul's voice. Paul expressed not only his concern and love for Sarah, but also his anger toward his father-in-law for what "he did to her," as well as frustration toward Sarah for not taking her medication.

This is not unusual. Many manic-depressive people have trouble staying on their medication. Like a lot of people struggling with a chronic illness, there are times when they like to deny its reality or severity.

Like diabetics who eat chocolate in order to push the fact of their disease away, manic-depressives will convince themselves they don't need medicine.

Some of them miss the mania part of their problem when it is controlled by medicine. Mania feels good—they believe they can do anything from hang gliding to writing the great American novel. In reality, all they accomplish is getting their families in trouble.

This is where support groups like the one David and Paul were in can be very helpful. Living with a manic-depressive is very hard. Paul loved Sarah but sadly admitted, "There are many times when I want to divorce her."

Unfortunately for Paul and Sarah, their story did not have a happy ending. Paul did eventually leave her, taking their three children with him. It was just too much for him to handle.

Before Paul and Sarah divorced she had been voluntarily or involuntarily committed multiple times. For many people just simply saying the words "mental hospital" strikes fear and terror.

Our society has painted inaccurate and unfair pictures of what it means to be a patient in the psychiatric ward of a hospital.

For spouses who have come to know the system, hospitalizations are a time of peace and renewed hope. For patients suffering with less debilitating or damaging mental problems, the hospital can be a safe haven for a time. Author William Styron, who suffered great bouts of depression, said:

> The hospital offers the mild, oddly gratifying trauma of sudden stabilization—a transfer out of the too familiar surroundings of home, where all is anxiety and discord, into an orderly and benign detention where one's only duty is to try to get well.[1]

If a loved one needs to go into the hospital for a time, it is important that family members understand the treatment plan. They should not be afraid to ask questions. Remember, this person is someone you love—he or she deserves the best care and attention.

Hospitalizations are not forever. They are also not a place for someone to go "for a rest." In truth, if a patient is following through with their whole treatment program, a lot of intensive work is accomplished. Rest comes in the fact that a person is taken out of a stressful environment for a while knowing he or she will need to return to it soon.

(For more information on hospital routines see the Appendix.)

"I'm Not the Monster I Thought I Was"

David completed the eight-week support group. Although he did not leave with a diploma or certificate in hand, he did feel he had graduated from an intensive course in understanding sexual abuse and the emotional illness it can cause.

At the last meeting the leader asked members to sum up the most important truths they learned during their time together. Each member of the group had a different angle or understanding.

"I'm not the monster I thought I was," said David, surprising himself by his own words. His biggest issues were his guilt and anger. The group enabled him to see that he was normal, that he was not alone, and that there were ways to deal with his feelings and still remain supportive of Elizabeth.

The poet John Donne said, "No man is an island, entire unto himself." This is true in the respect that no one is completely alone and that no one life can exist without touching another. Yet, each person has the capacity within him- or herself to create uncharted emotional islands. When we strive to keep distant and private, we have created an island where we try to find safety.

When families or individuals are racked with turmoil or illness, there is a tendency to allow these islands of safety to form. It is not until we build bridges that we can truly understand and accept ourselves and others—and to love each other in the way God intended. It is in our vulnerability and weakness that God's strength is quickened.

Whether it is in a formal setting, such as the group David attended, a close circle of friends, a single friend, or a small care group within a large church, support groups give the opportunity to build bridges and make connections that build up our strength and give us encouragement.

So We May Help Others

The desire to love, to care, support, and comfort is of God. In his second letter to the Corinthians, Paul described the circle of care:

> What a wonderful God we have—He is the Father of our Lord Jesus Christ, the source of every mercy, and the one who so wonderfully comforts and strengthens us in our hardships and trials. And why does He do this? So that when others are troubled, needing our sympathy and encouragement, we can pass on to them this same help and comfort God has given us (2 Corinthians 1:3-4).

This was the second valuable lesson David learned in his support group. He was not only better able to handle the stresses of Elizabeth's problems, but he was also equipped to help others who were in similar circumstances. This is the beauty of caring, the benefit of bearing one another's burdens. There is pleasure in helping another who has fallen. As King Solomon pointed out:

> If one falls, the other pulls him up; but if a man falls when he is alone, he's in trouble. . . . And one standing alone can be attacked and defeated, but two can stand back-to-back and conquer; three is even better, for a triple-braided cord is not easily broken (Ecclesiastes 4:10, 12).

Obviously, the idea of a support group is an old one. Sometimes the best way to help those we love the most is to find the help *we* need the most.

PART 3

Chapter Eleven
When Therapy Is Over

Saying good-bye is never easy. Yet life is filled with good-byes. We leave schoolyard friends and teachers behind as we grow and change. We leave our parents when we go away to school or make a home of our own.

Treasured toys and books and photographs that once meant so much are now gathering dust in the attic. We say tearful good-byes to brothers and sisters as they move on to new lives. We watch and wave as trusted friends take new positions and build new homes, promising to write and call, to stay in touch.

Leaving the people we love is part of life, and it is also part of recovery. In fact, it is another phase of the therapy process called termination. It sounds so final.

But how do you say good-bye to someone who may have saved your life, your marriage, your career, your friendships? How do you say good-bye to the person who helped you see beyond the pain and hurt into a bright future where anything is possible?

For weeks, months, or years, the therapist's office was a proving ground for all sorts of feelings and behaviors. It was a safe place to risk change. Then little by little those changes were incorporated into your loved one's life. Now it is time to risk those changes without the safety net provided by the therapist. This is the second task—meeting life and its challenges head-on and alone. Or so it may feel.

Who Can Say When It Is Time?

In earlier chapters we pointed out ways a family or individual can know when a loved one would benefit from professional counseling. We listed specific signs and symptoms that indicated a person was having trouble coping with daily life, or their mental health was deteriorating.

In the same way there are signposts that the family will notice along the road to recovery, pointing toward the finish line. In fact, these signs are just the opposite of the symptoms that the person brought into counseling.

Complaints of fatigue and body pain diminish as energy increases. No longer does the person commiserate with the psalmist who sang, "I am worn out with pain; every night my pillow is wet with tears" (Psalm 6:6).

Your spouse or friend now rejoices with the Apostle Paul who announced to the world, "I can do everything God asks me to with the help of Christ who gives me the strength and power" (Philippians 4:13).

There are other visible indications that life is getting better. Your loved one will take more pride in clothing and appearance. He or she will make better eye contact in conversation and be more open to outward displays of affection and love.

People who are emerging from the dark woods of depression into the light of wholeness say they are more observant, and see brighter colors than they ever did before. There is a greater awareness of the world around them and a desire to be part of it.

The person in the throes of depression or anxiety needs to stay home where it is safe. The recovering person desires more contact with people and begins participating in activities and social events. In general, they come alive and active.

The purpose of therapy is not to turn out perfect people, or eradicate the facts of suffering and struggle. The purpose of therapy is to give people like Elizabeth and her family new tools to better equip them to cope with those struggles and retain their alertness and desire to live life fully.

Determining when the time is right for the biggest change of all—flying solo—is generally a mutual decision that the client and therapist make together. In most cases, both have a sense that therapy is winding down. Medications have been decreased or stopped, frequency of visits has lessened, and the client generally feels less of a need to go to therapy. In a sense the patient outgrows the therapist.

This phase of therapy is a time of looking forward, not backward. It is a time of making plans for the future and getting comfortable with a newfound self. It all sounds so exciting, but it can also be sad for everyone.

The client is not the only person who feels a sense of loss when therapy ends. The doctor or counselor will experience feelings of separation in saying good-bye. A therapist invests a great deal of time, energy, and self in the patient or client. This goes back to what we discussed earlier about the therapist's need to be genuine and vulnerable. This kind of care doesn't come just from textbooks and lecture halls—it comes from the heart. It is a gift from God.

I cared about Elizabeth and felt sad when it was time to say good-bye. I had looked forward to seeing her and also watching her grow. There is a certain excitement that a therapist feels in seeing a patient accomplish a goal.

It is not unlike the feelings of a parent watching a child achieve and grow. I suppose this comes from the fact that everyone, regardless of age, has a child inside. It is with that child that much of the work of therapy is done. But it is still an adult relationship.

Long after a patient has left, I still remember and wonder how she or he is doing. And some patients stay connected by sending Christmas cards every year or checking in with me every few months. Connections can continue or the relationship can be severed completely.

Ambivalence

"Mama," said Anna, "do you have to go to the doctor tonight? Can't you please stay home? Just tonight?"

Elizabeth smiled at Anna. "I have to go to my appointment tonight, but guess what? I won't have to go out anymore this week."

David put his magazine down suddenly. "What?" he asked. "No more this week? Don't tell me she's going on vacation again."

Elizabeth laughed. "No. We just decided that I don't have to go so often. Once a week will be plenty. Then in a while we'll go to once a month, and pretty soon, no more therapy."

David sat quietly a moment. "Are you sure?" he said. "I mean it's a pretty big step. Are you sure it's time?"

Elizabeth laughed again. "You make it sound like I'm pregnant or something. Yes, I'm sure, we're sure. After three and one-half years, I don't think the doc would take any chances."

Changes made in therapy are both obvious and subtle. A formerly withdrawn, unassertive individual will one day participate in activities he or she would never have done before, or take charge of a situation usually left for someone else.

The change is rather like wearing new glasses. Some people notice right away. Others have to be told, and still others will figure it out on their own.

Many of the changes in Elizabeth's behaviors and moods were plainly seen. Once she was able to explore family secrets and hidden feelings, she and David grew closer. They enjoyed a more intimate relationship and made many improvements in their marriage which, in turn, affected their children.

But there were many internal changes in Elizabeth, changes that people would not be able to define but still would greatly benefit from. These changes made it possible for her to end the tradition of rage and volcanic anger inherited from her father.

Elizabeth began to take chances with the gifts and talents God gave her. She desired success, not failure. She had the will to go against the traditions of her family of origin, no longer allowing them to ensnare her.

Through therapy she decided which traditions she wanted to stop and which she wanted to pass on to her children. I saw Elizabeth and David begin new traditions of honesty and openness and start to create an environment in their home where feelings and ideas were discussed without ridicule or punishment.

The original problems that brought Elizabeth to see me had been resolved. When she looked in a mirror she no longer saw an ugly, weak monster staring back at her.

"I've been thinking about it for a while," said Elizabeth. "I just didn't want to say anything until I was certain. The doctor and I have been talking about it. She thinks cutting back on appointments is a good beginning to an ending."

"Well," said David, "now that you bring it up, I have noticed you don't get as many phone calls, and you did say you were cutting down on your medication. In fact, you actually seem, well, happy or something."

"Yeah," said Anna. "You don't holler anymore."

Elizabeth laughed. "I still holler," she said. "Just not as loud or as often."

Just then Daniel walked in bouncing a basketball. "Hey, Mom," he said. "Don't you have a shrinkfest tonight?"

"Don't bounce in the house," said David. "And yes, your mother is seeing the doctor. But guess what? She's going to be ending her therapy soon."

Daniel shot Elizabeth an incredulous glance. "No kidding?" he said. "We should have a party."

"Yeah," laughed David. "A coming out party."

Elizabeth's family met the decision for her to end therapy with cautious excitement. This is usually how it goes. Not only had Elizabeth become comfortable with therapy, but so had her family. They felt a certain safety while she was in counseling. But now that she was about to fly solo, they found themselves with mixed emotions and questions.

A Scary Time

Any new chapter in your life is a time of mixed feelings. Getting married, having babies, buying a house—any major event will create feelings of both excitement and trepidation. So, it was not unusual for Elizabeth and her family to view this time with ambivalence.

Once the decision has been made to end therapy and the client actually stops appointments, a spouse or other loved ones may become hypervigilant—watching every move, noticing every mood change. In a sense, watching and waiting for a relapse.

This happens to everyone. The wife of a former patient called me several weeks after her husband ended therapy. He had been having trouble sleeping, a symptom that originally brought him into therapy. The wife was frantic, convinced her husband was having a relapse.

But after we talked, she realized that what he was experiencing was normal, performance anxiety any musician would have before a concert—particularly if it was his first in two years.

It wasn't wrong for his wife to be concerned. No one wants to see someone they dearly love get tossed back into the maelstrom of depression and anxiety. Perhaps they believe that if it's caught soon enough, it can be corrected quickly.

Patients may have times of regression—dipping back into past maladaptive behaviors. The good news is that they realize this and cope with it. In fact, many patients become hypervigilant themselves, watching their every move.

It all comes back to trust . . . trust that changes are permanent, even if there is some waivering in behavior. Just as you and your loved one had to come to a place of trust within yourselves to make therapy work, now you must come to a place of trust with each other and with God.

"Stay always within the boundaries where God's love can reach and bless you" (Jude 1:21).

> I am sure that God who began the good work within you will keep right on helping you grow in His grace until His task within you is finally finished on that day when Jesus Christ returns (Philippians 1:6).

Chapter Twelve
Just When You Thought It Was Safe to Hold Hands Again

"Don't forget, my mother's coming for dinner tonight," said Elizabeth, as David left for work.

"Tonight?" he said. "So soon? This will be your first visit with her since you stopped therapy. Are you sure you're ready?"

Elizabeth laughed. "I have to do it sometime," she said. "Why not tonight? It will be all right."

David kissed Elizabeth. "I hope it goes well," he said.

During the last year of Elizabeth's therapy, she had kept visits with her mother at a minimum. They generally got together for holidays and birthdays, but most of their communication was over the phone.

Part of Elizabeth's growing process involved an acceptance of her mother for who she was—someone who would never love Elizabeth in the way she needed to be loved, or really know her in any meaningful way. This was hard for Elizabeth. She had missed having a mother she could count on, and she had always hoped that someday, somehow, her mother would become the person she so desperately wanted.

Finally, she could admit that it would never happen. And now, this dinner represented a time to try out her new convictions. She knew she would need to lean on David more to keep the conversation light. Although she had finished therapy, she still felt anxious at times and not completely confident in her new self.

After Elizabeth remembered her family secret, she wondered if her mother had known about it all along. And this made Elizabeth feel betrayed. But she knew she could never be the one to bring it up. There was always the chance that her mother did not know and would be devastated by the news.

Still, this gave Elizabeth a gnawing sense of disappointment. She believed her mother failed her, even if she didn't know. After all, couldn't she have sensed something was wrong as Elizabeth grew up? This was an anguish Elizabeth would probably carry the rest of her life.

The Visit

Even though her mother criticized the potatoes, Elizabeth and her family made it through dinner without a hitch. Elizabeth didn't crumble into a million pieces, and took comfort in the fact that David and the kids enjoyed the meal.

It was later, after her mother's favorite game show, that things started to turn sour. Elizabeth knew she was feeling fatigued and tried to compensate. But when her mother made Anna feel sad, she split wide open.

Anna had run into the living room waving a drawing. "Mama," she cried. "I did this at school. The teacher liked it so much she hung it on the bulletin board for the whole week."

Elizabeth took Anna in her arms and looked at her drawing. "It's lovely," she said. "I can see why your teacher was so pleased."

Just then, Elizabeth's mother snapped it out of her hands. "Oh this," she said crossly. "Your Aunt Katherine was doing amazing things at your age. In fact, she won all kinds of art awards."

Anna started to cry and took the drawing from her grandmother. She crumbled it into a ball and ran out of the room.

Elizabeth sat paralyzed. She wanted to speak. She knew she should, but nothing happened. All she could do was sit there and let her mother go on and on about how talented her sister Katherine was.

David managed to change the conversation without making it seem too obvious. After a few more minutes of mindless chatter, David took his mother-in-law home.

A Breakdown?

After her mother left, Elizabeth talked it over with Anna. She smoothed out her feelings, then her drawing, and hung it on the refrigerator.

"It doesn't matter what Grammy says. Your painting is wonderful. I love it, and I love you."

Anna shrugged. "Then why didn't you tell that to Grammy?"

Elizabeth felt tears stinging her eyes. Her stomach tightened like the rubber band inside a toy airplane. "I don't know," she sighed. "I thought I could handle her. Maybe nothing has changed."

Elizabeth put Anna to bed without a story or prayers. Just like the old days. "Mama's tired tonight," said Elizabeth. "Just go to sleep now."

Then Elizabeth made her way into her bedroom. She sat on the bed and sobbed. Once again her mother had gotten the best of her. Once again she had made her feel inadequate, not only her but her daughter.

I can't believe this, she thought. *I let everyone down. I'm no better than I was before. I failed Anna. I should have stood up for her.*

That night David tried to console Elizabeth. They discussed what happened and what should have happened. The next morning Elizabeth was still depressed. She was preoccupied and sorry for herself. The family felt Elizabeth's sadness, and they in turn were sad and confused.

"I knew it," declared Daniel. "Therapy didn't work. It didn't stick. She's depressed again."

"Be quiet, Daniel," demanded David. "It was a rough night. You missed it because of your ball game. Your mother has a right to feel sad. She'll pop out of it. The doctor said there would be times like this."

On the outside David was strong and in control. But inside his own nerves were shaken. He hadn't seen that look on Elizabeth's face in a long time. He worried that maybe she was relapsing, but he didn't want to leap to any conclusions. *I'll let her work it out,* he thought.

A week went by with no improvement. Elizabeth was still depressed. David knew something would have to be done.

"Look," he said finally. "I'm not sure, but I think you need to tell your mother what she did. Even if she can't understand, you have to tell her. Don't let her toss you backward like this. Take a stand. Go see her."

Elizabeth took a deep, shaky breath. "I know you're

right," she said. "But what good will it do? She'll never know how much she hurt me."

"What would the doctor tell you?" asked David.

Elizabeth thought a moment. "I guess she would tell me that my mother is a lost cause. That I should concentrate on the positive things around me, the people who really love me, like you and the kids. I guess she would tell me I had to guard Anna's feelings. I can't let Anna think I don't care."

"Then that's what you do. Whether she grasps it or not, you have to stand up for yourself and Anna. Remember what the doctor told us about breaking traditions? If you stand up to your mother, then Anna will get the message that it's okay to have feelings and that those feelings deserve to be heard."

Confrontation

At some point during or after therapy, a patient may decide to confront her perpetrator, the person(s) who damaged her life. This is best done after the client has had sufficient time to express and release her suppressed anger.

In her book *Partners in Recovery,* therapist Beverly Engel discusses confrontation.

> Confrontation can be either direct (meaning you involve the person you are confronting) or indirect (meaning that you don't). Whether she (he) chooses to confront directly or indirectly, the survivor will likely experience a tremendous amount of satisfaction when she stands up to those who hurt her and expresses her anger and pain. . . .
>
> Confronting is different from releasing anger in that its purpose is for survivors to stand up to those who hurt them in an assertive rather than angry fash-

> ion. Survivors are encouraged to rehearse their confrontation, or plan what they are going to say ahead of time, so they are able to say exactly what they want to say. Generally speaking, it is recommended that survivors include the following in their confrontation:
>
> 1. Exactly what the person did to them that caused them damage.
> 2. What effect the person's actions (or inaction) had on them, and how life has been affected.
> 3. What they would have wanted from the person at the time.
> 4. How they feel about the person now and what they want from them now.[1]

Although Ms. Engel's book is concerned with survivors of sexual abuse, her principles for confrontation are applicable to those who have been hurt in other ways. This includes adult children of alcoholics, victims of physical or verbal abuse, or neglect.

But confrontation is not for everyone. For many people it is just too scary to confront their abuser. For some it may even be dangerous. Confrontation must be very carefully planned, discussed, and prayed about. As we said earlier, confrontation is not a prerequisite to healing.

Many counselors are even advising against confrontation. Their belief is that it doesn't yield much except to arouse anger in family members, since most perpetrators do not admit their offense. Also, not all family members have been through counseling, and without this benefit, they would not be able to handle a confrontation in any kind of supportive or meaningful way.

Elizabeth was a victim of childhood incest. The fact that her perpetrator could not be confronted did not take away the offense. She still suffered and struggled to come to terms with his crime.

Also, Elizabeth had trouble with the fact that her mother was unwilling to admit to any knowledge of the incest, to help and protect her the way a mother should.

Obviously her mother still had a huge hold on Elizabeth's emotions and she played them like a guitar, plucking away at the strings until one snapped.

That is what happened the night of Elizabeth's dinner. When her mother hurt her and Anna in ways reminiscent of her childhood, Elizabeth immediately sank back into depression and anxiety. This time, however, there was a twist.

Because of the professional care she had received, Elizabeth was able to recognize what was happening and pull herself out of the crisis. She also knew that she had to stand up to her mother. But she was scared.

David watched Elizabeth's emotional status deteriorate. "It was like watching an instant replay," he said. "All of a sudden, over one conversation she was back in the pits. All I could think about was that we had just wasted all those years and money on therapy that didn't work. But then I realized that my mother-in-law could not be that powerful. She could be stopped. Elizabeth knew this too."

It is not unusual for someone just getting out of therapy to have times of regression. Sometimes it takes only one, seemingly simple experience to send the person hurtling backward. But if therapy was successful, setbacks won't last long, and the person will find the courage to use the tools she learned in therapy to combat the forces within and without.

"Mom, We Have to Talk"

It took Elizabeth more than a week to swim up from the new depression. "It wasn't like before," she said. "This time I knew somewhere in the back of my mind that I could beat it. Even though I was tempted to get on the phone with the doc, I resisted. Suddenly it was very important for me to do it alone. It seems strange to think of the many times I couldn't even make a simple decision without first consulting my doctor."

Elizabeth had set a meeting with her mother. Its purpose was not to dump all of Elizabeth's negative feelings from childhood, adolescence, and adulthood. Her mother would never understand, accept, or even allow that.

Elizabeth's purpose was singular. She wanted to stand up to her mother about what happened at dinner. Elizabeth decided to focus on a new beginning, not on the past, even though she would always carry around the misgiving that her mother could have helped when Uncle Richard was abusing her.

This was time for setting new boundaries, protecting herself and her family from the dysfunctional ways of the past.

"Mom, we need to talk," said Elizabeth, after she arrived at her mother's home.

"Of course, dear," said her mother. "Did I leave my glass case at your house the other night? I can't find it anywhere."

Elizabeth rolled her eyes. "Mom, I don't know. We'll look for it. Right now I have something to say—about dinner the other night."

"Oh, it was very good. The potatoes were a little salty, but . . . "

"Mother," Elizabeth interrupted, "let me talk."

Elizabeth's mother squirmed in her chair. "Okay, dear, talk. What's on your mind?"

Elizabeth took a deep breath. "I'm here to tell you that I didn't appreciate the way you treated me or Anna the other night. You had no business insulting my daughter like that. She was very hurt."

"But, Lizzie, what did I say?"

"And please don't call me Lizzie. You compared Anna with Katherine, me with Katherine, Van Gogh with Katherine. It wasn't right. Anna's drawing was good and needed to be recognized for itself."

"O Elizabeth, I didn't mean anything. It's just that I'm so proud of all my girls, it's hard not to compare."

"Mom, that's really twisted. We're each our own person; we each have our own talents."

"I didn't think I did anything so bad. What am I, a terrible person now? A monster?"

"Don't start with the guilt trip, Mom. I'm talking about one thing. The next time you upset Anna or compare me with Katherine, I'm going to ask you to leave. I can't allow it anymore."

Elizabeth felt her heart leap into her throat. Her palms were sweating, and she thought she would hyperventilate.

"Well," said her mother. "I'll never mention Katherine's name in your presence again."

Elizabeth had to fight the urge to buy into her mother's pity party. She resisted. "It would be good if I left now. I'll call in a couple of days. We'll plan another dinner, okay?"

"Well, I still don't understand the problem," said her mother, continuing to egg her on.

"I know," answered Elizabeth. "Just remember what I said. And I'm quite serious."

Elizabeth gathered her handbag and started out the door. "Mom," she said turning around, "I came here and said these things because I love Anna. And you know, for the first time in my life I can say this—I came today because I love myself."

Elizabeth managed to keep back the tears until she reached her car. She drove a little way down the street and then stopped to have a good cry.

New Traditions

Elizabeth started a new tradition by standing up to her mother. She wasn't angry or hostile. She asserted her needs and stuck to her convictions even when tempted to crumble. Elizabeth confronted her mother and set a new boundary line. There was no way of knowing when or if her mother would cross it, but Elizabeth had every intention of abiding by her own new rules. When she arrived home she told Anna what she had done. Anna received the respect she deserved and learned she could be her own person.

Later that evening, I received a call from Elizabeth. She was tearful, yet hopeful. She told me what had happened. I was proud of her. I knew how tough it was for her to confront her mother. I remembered when Elizabeth couldn't make a simple exchange at a department store. She had grown. And now because of her new strength, her family would grow as well.

Elizabeth had had a small setback and spiraled into depression, but she had lifted herself out and put herself on the right track.

Fortunately, this story had a good ending or, more appropriately, a good beginning. Elizabeth discovered truths about herself and her family of origin that were ugly and marred, possibly by generations of maladaptive behavior and belief systems.

The act of standing up to her mother was just one of many new and healthy behaviors Elizabeth would develop. She didn't pop out of therapy ready to take a bite out of the world. She was at the beginning of a new life, new traditions, healthier relationships with God, her family, and her friends. She would always need time to grow. But now she could meet the conflicts with less trepidation.

This is the goal of therapy or counseling—to put the three rings back into a harmony consistent with biblical beliefs and goals, allowing a person to live a more balanced life.

Chapter Thirteen
David's Story Five Years Later

Elizabeth ended therapy almost five years ago. I wish I could say we all lived happily ever after. That may happen in fairy tales, but life is not a fairy tale and "happily ever after" takes a lot of hard work.

I'll never forget that first horrible night eight years ago when Elizabeth jumped out of bed screaming and begging me to leave. When I tried to hold her, to comfort her she pushed me away. "Please leave," she cried. "I can't be with you." That was scary. I thought she had lost her mind. But then I thought it was just a nightmare and everything would be fine the next day. It wasn't.

We saw our family physician. He said she needed a psychiatrist. Talk about a bomb dropping. All of a sudden it seemed like my world was crumbling right in front of me, and there was nothing I could do to stop it.

I was told Elizabeth was mentally ill. Oh, they used phrases like panic disorder and depression—a word reserved also for small dents in cars or mild tropical storms. What I didn't know then was that although my life was all of a sudden shattering, Elizabeth's life had shattered when she was just a child. She had been trying to compensate, to be as healthy and happy as possible; but as in any ill-conceived battle, she lost.

Like any Christian man, I prayed for Elizabeth's mental health. I figured if I couldn't talk about it, maybe I could pray, but that wasn't so simple. I prayed and prayed—every day all day, sometimes to the point of tears. Elizabeth just sank deeper and deeper in depression. Soon she couldn't even go shopping, the panic attacks were so awful.

Then a friend showed me something that C.S. Lewis wrote:

> Some things are proved by the unbroken uniformity of our experiences. The law of gravitation is established by the fact that, in our experience, all bodies without exception obey it. Now even if all the things that people prayed for happened, which they do not, this would not prove what Christians mean by efficacy of prayer. For prayer is request, as distinct from compulsion, in that it may or may not be granted.[1]

In other words, just because I asked didn't mean I would receive. But I would like to add something. Sometimes the granting of the prayer takes time, and sometimes we have to go through a series of tests and trials before God gives us what we asked for.

For us it was over four years of intense therapy, support groups, school counselors, supportive friends, and church and, of course, the knowledge that God was right there with us slowly pulling us through the waters. Isaiah writes:

> Don't be afraid, for I have ransomed you; I have called you by name; you are Mine. When you go through deep waters and great trouble, I will be with you. When you go through rivers of difficulty, you will not drown! When you walk through the fire of oppression, you will not be burned up—the flames will not consume you (Isaiah 43:1-2).

"Rivers of difficulty." I laugh now, but a few years ago our river made the white waters of the Colorado look like a trout stream. There were times when I thought the marriage would have to end. Elizabeth was always so depressed or so angry or so something that I just couldn't take it anymore. All I could think about was protecting my own sanity and my kids. That was usually when I called the doc or a friend and got hold of myself.

I had to think about Elizabeth and the terrible things she went through. And how she had the courage to go through it all again, this time to gain understanding, to learn who she was so angry with. Therapy is tough. It's like reliving your life and discovering that all the ways you learned to adapt and cope are wrong and unhealthy.

I wasn't perfect, far from it, in fact. It was hard on me in a lot of ways. There were days when I didn't even want to come home from work, because I didn't know who would be waiting—the depressed, sullen Elizabeth or the angry, hostile Elizabeth yelling and screaming at everybody.

Eventually things started getting better. When her doctor finally found the right medication for her, life improved. Elizabeth improved, even in little ways that came to mean a lot. Like getting laundry done, cooking meals, really caring for the kids in special Mom ways. That gave me hope. And when you're going through something as dramatic as all this, all you can really count on is hope. Hope in each other to stay committed, no matter what; hope in the doctor or therapist; and, most importantly, hope in Jesus Christ.

What Is the Hope of Jesus Christ?

The word *hope,* in one form or another, appears over 150 times in Scripture. In each case it means basically the same thing—"to wait, to be patient and trust." The writers of the Bible use the word *hope* to increase courage and joy, to speak of salvation and assurance, to find stability and patience. I guess you could say that when the going gets tough, the tough hope. Without it there would have been no future for Elizabeth, and without Elizabeth I shudder to think about my future.

Elizabeth has a favorite poem taped to the refrigerator. She put it up about a year after she started seeing the doctor.

> "Hope" is the thing with feathers
> That perches in the soul,
> And sings the tune without the words,
> And never stops at all,
>
> And sweetest in the gale is heard;
> And sore must be the storm
> That could abash the little bird
> That kept so many warm.
>
> I've heard it in the chillest land,
> And on the strangest sea;
> Yet, never, in extremity,
> It asked a crumb of me.

Emily Dickinson[2]

We never lost hope. Even when the storms came and threatened to destroy our home, we had hope. I can't help but think of the myth of Pandora's box. When she opened it, she unleashed terrible miseries on the earth. What many people forget is that at the bottom of Pandora's box was hope.

Therapy is like that. Elizabeth unleashed all kinds of problems, but she still had hope; and when she didn't have hope, I did; and when I didn't, the doctor did. That is what is meant in Ecclesiastes by a chord of three strings.

But what about God? Now that's a tough question. Although I never doubted God's presence with us, I did question His wisdom and, I'm embarrassed to say, His sanity in allowing us to go through such terrible times. Again I had to keep going back to Scripture to find places where God allowed calamity to strike, and hardship to befall His people. I read how He brought them through it, as He brought the Israelites into the Promised Land. He did, after all, promise. So why wouldn't He deliver us?

He promised us as well that He would never leave us or forsake us. He promised that all things will somehow work for good. Elizabeth had a hard time believing all this.

Our Earthly Fathers

According to Elizabeth's doctor, our pastor, and countless other people, a person's perception of God is colored by what kind of relationship they had with their parents—especially fathers.

Elizabeth's father was abusive and unloving and totally without affection. It's easy to see how she came to believe in a God who would punish her without reason and who couldn't possibly love her. Elizabeth grew up believing she was unlovable.

People whose parents neglected them naturally see a God of neglect and disinterest. Kids with tyrannical fathers see God as a taskmaster, or puppet master pulling strings at will.

Once Elizabeth was able to work through her past and see herself as lovable, she was able to change her view of God. But it didn't just happen—snap! It took a long time. Even now, five years later, Elizabeth questions God's love at times and wonders if He really cares or if He's going to punish her somehow.

The difference now is that she doesn't dwell on her concerns. She sees God more clearly. It is as though all the love passages in Scripture were blurred to Elizabeth's eyes. She never saw them. Now she reads with excitement and shares God's love with me and the children. Getting to know God is a lifelong endeavor. We never stop discovering Him.

John Calvin said, "The more we know of ourselves the more we know God, and the more we know God the more we know of ourselves." Knowledge is on a continuum.

God made men and women to have relationships. It is one thing to desire a time of being alone with your thoughts, a book, a painting or a project. But no one really wants to be lonely. God just didn't intend it that way. That is why therapy is not a solitary journey. Oh, there were many times when I felt left out. But that was when I learned the difference between privacy and secrecy.

When Elizabeth started telling me the family secrets she carried around, well, that was when I learned about patience and long-suffering. And that was when I learned that professing Jesus Christ as Savior does not automatically guard us from struggles and sorrow.

In This World

The Bible says we are in the world but not of it. By virtue of the fact that we stand on planet earth, we are vulnerable to its pains and sorrows and joys.

Jesus said His disciples would have trouble and trials *in* this world. But He would deliver them, either on earth or in heaven. Elizabeth was one of the fortunate ones. Through counseling, prayer, and loving support, she unlocked the stranglehold of depression. She came through the deepest parts of an emotional dark woods.

It may be hard to accept that not everyone is delivered from the plagues of this world. The Book of Hebrews puts it in grizzly terms:

> Some were laughed at and their backs cut open with whips, and others were chained in dungeons. Some died by stoning and some by being sawed in two; others were promised freedom if they would renounce their faith, then were killed with the sword. Some went about in skins of sheep and goats, wandering over deserts and mountains, hiding in dens and caves. They were hungry and sick and ill-treated—too good for this world. And these men of faith, though they trusted God and won His approval, none of them received all that God had promised them; for God wanted them to wait and share the even better rewards that were prepared for us (Hebrews 11:36-40).

God Is Good

Watching someone you love go through therapy is tough. Some days you feel like it will never end. Then it finally does and you have times of wishing it wasn't over. There was a certain security in therapy. Now we had to handle crises by ourselves. But, I can honestly say that in the last five years there may have been only a dozen times when I really wished Elizabeth was still in therapy or wondered if she should be. That's twelve days out of one thousand eight hundred and twenty-five—not bad.

God is good. He promised to be right there with us, even after therapy. He was and always will be, now in even brighter ways. Elizabeth has turned her relationship with God into a working relationship. I admire her strength and her devotion. It is obvious that her trials dug the groundwork for a healthy, wonderful walk with God. And it has rubbed off on me and the kids.

When Elizabeth's therapy ended, I had to wonder, *Where does she go from here?* I appreciated the immediate changes. We could sleep together, she didn't fly off the handle as easily, she was more friendly, and she had a greater desire to know and love God.

She was more assertive, in positive ways. I mean she didn't devour the mailman when he was late. She set her mother straight on some things. She even finished projects she started years earlier.

Still, where do you go after therapy? The answer, I believe, lies in your relationships. Particularly the one you have with God. Anything can happen in human relationships. The only true, stable, and forever love of your life is God. That I believe is where you go after recovery—to the Cross, taking hold of the truth that Jesus came so that we might have life, and have it more abundantly (John 10:10).

APPENDIX

So Much Information

We live in an Age of Information. Lost in the Mall? Go to Information. Can't find a book? Go to the information table. Even telephone books offer great quantities of information—like evacuation plans in case of a nuclear accident.

Today's home computers can be linked all across the country to form huge networks of information on virtually any subject, from medical advice to fixing a leaky faucet to the most popular parenting techniques.

But yet, with all the information and resources available, it is sad to think of the number of people who go without physical, psychological, and spiritual help.

In the following pages we are going to provide more

information, about your mind and how it works, about what can go wrong and who is qualified to fix it. You will find information on the best psychiatric medications—how they work and what side effects you can expect. Such information could save a life, or a mind, or a family.

Consider for a minute the miraculous gifts that God imparted to us all at the moment He breathed life into Adam . . . the ability to think and wonder and dream, to feel and grow.

Isn't the gift of language incredible? God has given us ways to express ourselves that none of His other creatures possess. Think of the creative spirit through which we paint and draw and write and make music and dance.

In His wisdom and grace, God has provided resources to help us understand and use these gifts in ways that will enable us to reach ever higher in our quest to be more like Him.

Psychology is one of these resources. It is the psychiatrist, the psychologist, social worker, counselor, and pastor who attempt to explore these gifts and help us to reach the full potential hidden within.

The pages that follow are another resource for those who love someone struggling with the gift of self.

WHO ARE THE COUNSELORS?

Name	Degree(s)	Credentials
Psychiatrist	M.D. or D.O.	Four years of medical school. Four years of psychiatric residency. Licensed to evaluate for medication and hospitalization. May be trained in various techniques of psychotherapy. May be Board Certified. Must pass all national and state examinations to qualify.
Psychologist	Ph.D.	Four years of college. Four to six years of doctoral training. One year of internship in order to perform psychological testing and various techniques of therapy. Must pass state examinations.
Psychologist	M.A.	Four years of college. Two years of post-graduate schooling and intern program. State licensed.
Pastoral Counselor	M.A. Ph.D.	Some seminaries offer post-college degrees in pastoral counseling.
Certificate Programs		Programs of various lengths of study and supervision aimed at a specific problem such as alcohol addiction.

HOW DO THEY COUNSEL?

Type of Therapy Or Counseling	Their View of the Origin Of Problems
Family Systems	Family is a system characterized by 1. Organization. 2. Interrelatedness. 3. Interaction of members. 4. Control mechanisms. 5. Tendencies toward stability and/or change. A disturbance on any level of the system presents a problem.
Biological	Emotional problems are due to changes in the chemistry of the nervous system and result in biochemical imbalances.
Psychodynamic	Emotional problems are due to feelings, conflicts, and distortions of the past that have been repressed in the unconscious mind.
Behavioral/ Cognitive	Causes of behavior are sought in the person's environment rather than in psyche. Behavior is thought to be learned, predictable, and controllable.
Humanistic	Problems are due to a person not actualizing his or her full potential or real self.
Pastoral	Provides various psychological, social, spiritual, and material support.

SUICIDE

The **SAD PERSONS** Scale for Assessing the Risk of Suicide

Sex	Is the person male or female? Females attempt suicide more often than males. Males succeed more often than females.
Age	Is the person a teenager or senior citizen?
Depression	Has the person been suffering depression?
Previous Attempt	Has the person ever made an attempt?
Evidence of alcohol or drug abuse	Is there a history of substance abuse?
Rational thinking lost	Are there any psychotic symptoms?
Social supports lacking	Does the person lack friends, relatives, or support from church or employment?
Organized plan	Does the person have a well-defined, lethal method available?
No spouse	Is the person widowed, divorced, single, or separated?
Sickness	Has the person been suffering from chronic, debilitating, or serious illness?

As a general rule, the more *yes* answers, the greater the risk for suicide. Do not be afraid to ask your loved one if he or she is thinking about committing suicide.[1]

There are many myths that surround this difficult subject; they only plunge it further underground.

Myth: If you talk about it, you will plant the seed in the person's mind.

Truth: The thought is already there and the person may feel ignored or unimportant if you don't ask. Some people caught up in depression could interpret your silence as a signal to go ahead and do it.

Myth: A person must be "out of his mind" to commit suicide.

Truth: The person can be very rational with a well-conceived plan.

Myth: Suicide always happens without warning.

Truth: Eighty percent of people who attempt suicide give some kind of prior warning.

Myth: Suicide is an inherited tendency.

Truth: There is no genetic predisposition to it.

Myth: Being a Christian protects you from suicidal thoughts.

Truth: Some Christians commit suicide.

Myth: When the crisis is over, the danger is gone.

Truth: Although they may behave calmly, they can still be planning suicide. Often the calm after the storm is a signal that they have made a decision.

QUESTIONS TO ASK A SUICIDAL PERSON

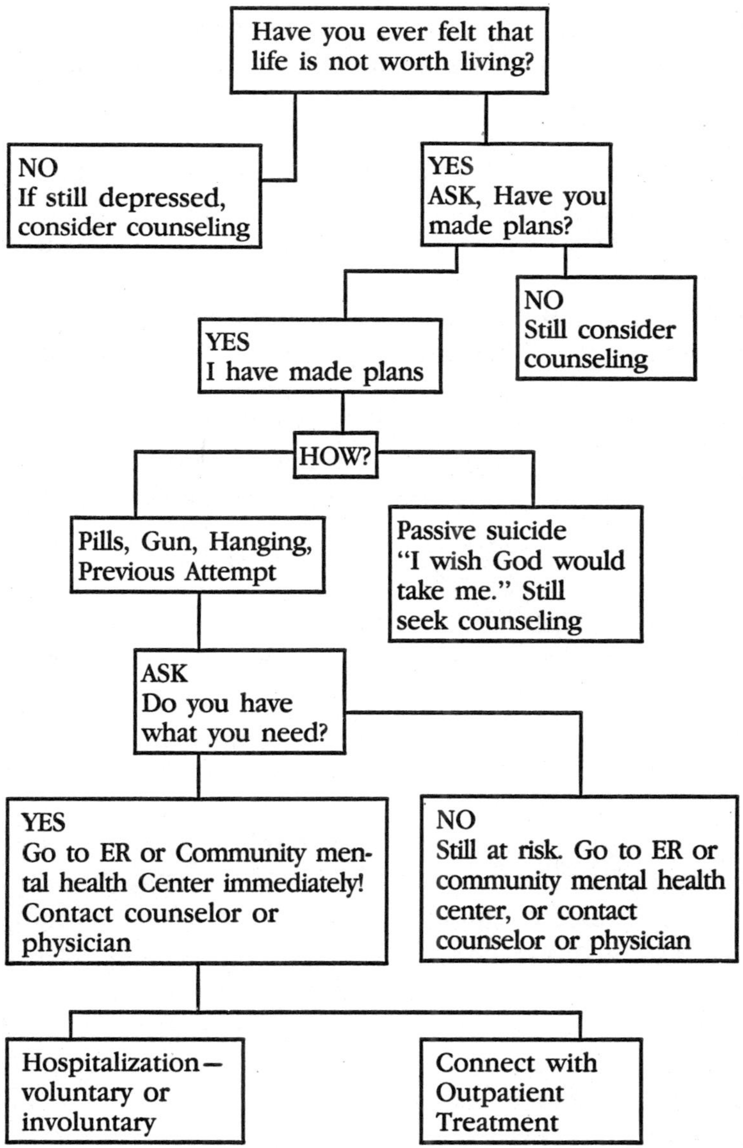

WHAT DOES IT MEAN TO BE COMMITTED?

In 1963 the United States Government passed the Community Mental Health Act. This act provided for inpatient, outpatient, partial hospitalization, emergency room and other auxiliary services for people in need, regardless of their ability to pay. These services are provided to people at geographically defined Catchment Areas.

Involuntary Commitment is an act of civil legislation. Doctors or other mental health professionals cannot, on their own, commit a patient. A person cannot be committed against his wishes without state government approval and/or intervention.

Mental health professionals must follow a system of checks and balances before anyone can be ordered into a hospital. The procedure for involuntary commitment is as follows:

1. The therapist sees probable cause for commitment.
2. The therapist must complete special petition forms.
3. The therapist then calls the court adjudicator for approval.
4. The therapist then calls the police and the person is taken to the hospital emergency room.
5. The patient is evaluated by another doctor. If he or she agrees that commitment is necessary, the patient is taken by police or ambulance to a mental health facility.
6. Within three days, the patient is granted a hearing before a judge. If the judge agrees that hospitalization is necessary, a twenty-day commitment is authorized.
7. After the twenty-day commitment time is over and doctors still agree the patient needs further care but refuses to comply, the patient is again brought before a

judge who will issue another twenty-day commitment authorization.

No one can be committed indefinitely. The system is not designed to "lock people away."

The three reasons for Involuntary Commitment are expressed in these questions. A yes answer to any question could lead to commitment.

1. In the last thirty days, has the person attempted self-harm, either by attempted suicide or self-mutilation?
2. In the last thirty days, has the person attempted to hurt someone else? Is this person homicidal?
3. In the last thirty days, has the person shown inability to care for his own needs, e.g., proper hygiene, dressing, eating?

If a person refuses hospitalization, a spouse or other person may go to the Community Mental Health Center or Emergency Room and request an emergency involuntary examination. Then the professionals will follow the above steps to assure the best care for the patient.

While hospitalization may be necessary in some cases, the days of "snake pits" are gone. Hospitals are geared toward helping and genuinely caring for mentally ill people. For some of them, the hospital is a kind of "rest stop." The order and routine, the built-in structure of the hospital, can be very reassuring and produce a stabilizing effect in a deeply anxious or depressed person.

Once a patient has been admitted to the hospital, he or she is evaluated by a psychiatrist and the nursing staff. A suicidal patient will be kept under close observation until the treatment team decides otherwise.

Generally, the hospital stay will include a full medical evaluation, including blood and urine tests. This is important because so many physical conditions can cause or mimic certain psychological symptoms, including depression and anxiety.

The inpatient treatment team includes the psychiatrist who will act as head of the team, the nursing staff, a psychologist, and a social worker. Depending on the course of treatment, other professionals could be involved, including art and music therapists.

Family members should be well advised of treatment plans and stay in close contact with one member of the team. Usually the social worker is responsible for family contact, but it is also appropriate to speak with the psychiatrist.

Patients generally wear street clothes and participate in as many activities as the team allows or advises. The day usually begins with a patient meeting. This is where the patient community gathers to discuss any problems or concerns with the nursing staff.

In some hospitals it is the patient community that helps decide whether another patient's privileges may be advanced. Then the patients disperse for various activities or meetings, including individual therapy, group therapy, art or music therapy, or other social and physical activities.

Family members are encouraged to visit. As treatment progresses, the patient will have more privileges and be able to go off the ward or outside the hospital, depending on safety restrictions. Privileges include day or weekend passes, allowing the patient to spend time with family members away from the hospital.

MAJOR PSYCHOLOGICAL SYMPTOMS

It would be impossible to list all the possible mental illnesses and their symptoms. Many illnesses involve a combination of different symptoms which will overlap with a specific diagnosis.

For example, someone who is suffering from a major depression may also be exhibiting signs of anxiety disorder or have occasional psychotic episodes.

On the following pages we have outlined the major symptoms and illness.[2]

ANXIETY

Anxiety is characterized by an intense sense of impending doom or disaster. It is the major symptom of the following illnesses.

Panic Disorder may occur with or without agoraphobia. Panic disorders are marked by panic attacks. A person suffering from this will periodically experience shortness of breath, dizziness, heart palpitations, sweating, nausea, numbness, flushes, chest pain, hyperventilation, and the fear of dying.

Phobias are persistent, irrational fears of a specific object, activity or situation that compel a person to avoid them. Although he knows that his fear is out of proportion to the actual danger, the patient cannot control it or explain it away. For example, a claustrophobic person fears closed-in places like closets, elevators, or caves. Phobias are marked by anticipatory anxiety including profuse sweating, poor motor control, rapid pulse, and elevated blood pressure.

Generalized Anxiety Disorder is characterized by excessive worry over life's circumstances, without apparent good reason. It is marked by vigilance, always being on the lookout for real or imagined danger. The person will experience heightened muscle tension and increased activity of the involuntary nervous system, resulting in conditions such as irritable bowel syndrome or stomach ulcers. Age of onset varies but usually occurs between twenty and forty.

Posttraumatic Stress Syndrome is a condition resulting from trauma considered outside the normal range of human experience; for example, rape, incest, war experiences. PTS is marked by flashbacks and anxiety when exposed to events or objects that resemble the initial trauma. Other symptoms include insomnia, difficulty in falling asleep, nightmares about the traumatic event, aggressive outbursts upon waking, chronic anxiety, and panic attacks.

Obsessive-Compulsive Disorder is an anxiety occurring when obsessions and compulsions are blocked. An obsession is a recurrent idea, thought, or image. A compulsion is a repetitive, ritualistic, and involuntary defensive behavior in response to internal rules.

This disease causes significant distress and may impair occupational and social functions. It is generally chronic with remissions and flare-ups. The prognosis is better than average when symptoms are quickly identified, diagnosed, and treated.

Atypical Depression is an agitation, anxiety and preoccupation with bodily sensations often resulting in hypochondria.

DEPRESSION

Feelings of sadness and discouragement are part of daily life. But there are times when depression is more than just having the blues. Depression is a cause for concern when it is characterized by these feelings becoming more intense, pervasive, and persistent. People suffering from depression will have a decreased interest in pleasurable activities, changes in appetite (usually weight loss), sleep disturbances (generally insomnia), fatigue, poor concentration, feelings of worthlessness, hopelessness, profound feelings of guilt, and thoughts of death and suicide.

Secondary Depression arises during the course of physical or mental illness. For example, side effects of medications, infectious diseases, dementia, hypothyroidism or other endocrine diseases, and postpartum depression.

Primary Depression is unlike a secondary depression. People suffering with a primary depression will have no evidence of physical illness. Major depression occurs in about 10 percent of all Americans, regardless of race, sex, or socioeconomic group.

Manic-Depression or Bipolar Depression is characterized by extreme shifts in mood, swinging from depression to mania or euphoria. A person locked in the manic episode of the disease will have a persistent euphoric or elevated mood, feelings of grandiosity, decreased need for sleep, increased talkativeness, racing thoughts, and extreme distractibility, often colorful and flamboyant behavior. The patient will participate in activities that feel pleasurable without considering the consequences, e.g., driving too fast, spending money, increased sexual activity. The patient will go back and forth between the two extremes.

Manic-depression is common to both men and women. It is more common in higher socioeconomic groups and is associated with high levels of creativity and intelligence. It begins any time after adolescence, with first attacks usually occurring between ages twenty and thirty-five.

PSYCHOSIS

The psychotic person has a level of disorganized thinking that makes it impossible to distinguish between reality and fantasy, or differentiate information that comes from the outside world and the inside world. Psychosis can be manifested in depression, mania, and organic delusional syndromes. It can be induced by amphetamines, PCP, or LSD. Psychotic symptoms can be transient, such as a brief reactive psychosis.

Schizophrenia is a mental illness beginning in late adolescence that manifests itself in psychotic thinking, social withdrawal, marked impairment of personal hygiene, and lessened ability to work. The person with schizophrenia has a very restricted capacity to show feelings through facial expressions. Patients have delusions, hallucinations, and incoherence in speech and thought. It is generally a life-long chronic illness that can be managed through medication.

Schizophrenia is not the same as split personality or multiple personality. Schizophrenia has several subcategories: Catatonic, Paranoid, Disorganized, and Undifferentiated.

EATING DISORDERS

People with an eating disorder exhibit a gross disturbance in eating behavior and in their attitude toward self and food.

Anorexia Nervosa (Restrictive) is an illness in which people refuse to maintain a weight considered minimally normal for persons of that age and height. Patients will lose weight and maintain it at 15 percent below normal, because of their intense fear of becoming fat. Although they may be extremely underweight, they will perceive themselves as being fat, even when looking in a mirror.

This disorder primarily affects adolescent females and young women, but is not uncommon among older women; it does occasionally affect males.

Prognosis varies but is improved if the diagnosis is made early or if patients voluntarily ask for help and desire to overcome the illness. Anorexia nervosa has the highest mortality associated with a psychiatric disturbance.

Bulimia Nervosa is characterized by recurrent bouts of uncontrollable binge eating, followed by self-induced vomiting, use of laxatives or diuretics, strict dieting, and vigorous exercise to prevent weight gain. These patients have an overpreoccupation with body shape and weight. This disorder primarily affects young women.

Overeating The compulsion to overeat can be as debilitating and problematic as the compulsion to undereat. These patients have a persistent, emotionally based pattern for overeating. It can be characterized by night eating, binge eating, or exacerbated by stress. These patients are sedentary, chew less, and eat more rapidly than others.

PERSONALITY DISORDERS

Someone with a personality disorder has observable and predictable patterns of day-to-day behavior. A disorder is marked by an inflexible and maladaptive way of perceiving, of relating to and thinking about the world, and oneself. Such persons rarely feel distressed or anxious about their behavior, and tend to blame others for their problems. People with personality disorders rarely receive treatment; and if they do, they are seen as outpatients.

Paranoid persons exhibit a pervasive, unwarranted tendency to interpret the actions of others with ill will and as threatening. They continually question others' loyalty, fidelity, and trustworthiness. Other identifying symptoms include poor self-image, social isolation, hostility, poor sense of humor, and jealousy.

Schizoid behavior is characterized by a pervasive indifference to others in relationships. The schizoid personality has a restricted range of emotions. This results in a high degree of social isolation.

Schizotypal persons display eccentricities of appearance, speech, and ideas. Their inability to relate to others results in social isolation.

Avoidant patients have a fearful avoidance of persons and situations where there is a perceived risk of failure, rejection, or strong emotional arousal. Although they are painfully shy and self-effacing, they have a strong desire for relationships.

Dependent persons have a pattern of extreme submissiveness, seeking and accepting directions from others, and displaying a persistent need for reassurance. They will exhibit an inability to be alone, easy suggestibility, lack of perseverance, and feelings of inferiority and self-doubt.

Passive-Aggressive behavior is marked by covert noncompliance and passive resistance to the reasonable demands of everyday social and work performance. Procrastination is a primary symptom of this personality disorder. Other symptoms include chronic lateness, fear of authority, forgetfulness, covert hostility or anger, and complaining and blaming behavior.

Narcissistic patients view themselves in a grandiose way, with an unrealistic overevaluation of their own importance and achievements. These patients have an extreme need for attention and will come across as arrogant and entitled. Their relationships are shallow, unempathetic, and will continue only as long as other people provide a source of admiration.

Antisocial behavior is marked by a lack of a moral sense of right and wrong. The antisocial person has a chronic disregard for the rights of others, evasion of financial obligations, chronic lying, and lack of fidelity and loyalty. Promiscuity, repeated substance abuse, illegal activity, fighting, child abuse, and the inability to plan for the future are other indications of an antisocial personality.

Obsessive-Compulsive behavior is marked by obsessive preoccupation with mental and interpersonal control and orderliness, at the expense of flexibility and ability to have fun. There is a restricted expression of warm and tender feelings. Obsessive-compulsives are often stingy, obstinate, and indecisive.

Histrionic persons use overly expressive actions, appearances, and feelings to evoke and maintain the interest and admiration of others. They are often colorful, dramatic, extroverted, and flirtatious. Their emotions have a superficial and insincere quality. They crave attention, are manipulative and divisive, and exhibit dramatic, emotional, or erratic behavior and thinking.

Borderline personalities suffer from a constant fear of and intolerance for being alone. They have sustained feelings of loneliness, emptiness, and rage; their unstable, fluctuating moods often result in impulsive self-destructive acts. Their relationships are unstable and are marked by manipulation, devaluation, and dependency.

Masochistic behavior is marked by continued involvement in avoidable, self-defeating behaviors, and relationships in which they complain of being victimized. There is a lack of pleasure, an avoidance of success, and a prevailing sense that no matter what they do, their life will be full of misery.

MEDICATIONS

The brain has various focal centers that regulate emotions. These centers are filled with thousands of nerve cells (neurons) that transmit emotional information from one nerve to the other.

This is accomplished through complex chemicals (proteins) called neurotransmitters. An overproduction or underproduction of these chemicals affects a person's emotional stability. These chemical imbalances are caused by:

1. Hormones—thyroid, estrogen, steroids
2. Stress
3. Prescription and nonprescription drugs
4. Physical illness

Four commonly recognized neurotransmitters are believed to play a large part in certain mental illnesses.

NAME	BALANCE	ILLNESS
Serotonin	Not enough	Depression O.C.D.
Norepinephrine	Not enough	Depression
Dopamine	Too much	Psychosis
GABA	Too much	Anxiety

The nerve cells manufacture the protein neurotransmitter, such as Serotonin. The protein is stored in a reservoir. When it is triggered to transmit information, the reservoir releases the neurotransmitter into the microscopic space between the two nerves.

The neurotransmitter (Serotonin) can do one of three things. It can:

The Nerve Cell

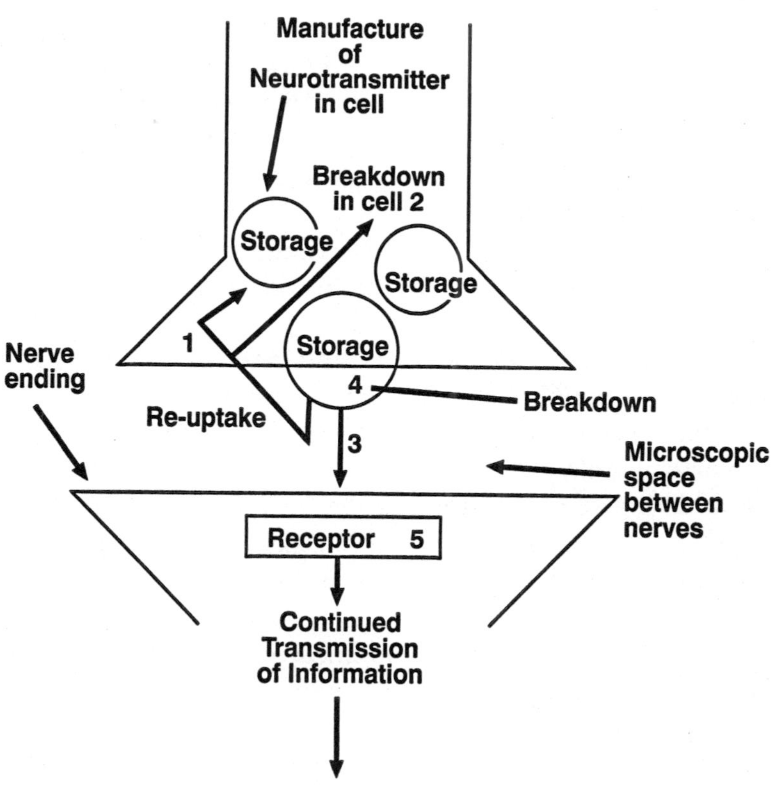

1. Trigger the next cell to transmit the information.
2. Be broken down or remetabolized outside the cell.
3. Be reabsorbed back into the cell for storage or breakdown.

HOW DO MEDICATIONS AFFECT THE NERVE CELLS?

Antidepressants—TCA	1. Blocks re-uptake of neurotransmitter (see diagram)
MAO Inhibitors	2. Blocks monamineoxadase and its breakdown
ECT (Electro-convulsive therapy)	3. Causes rapid release of neurotransmitter
Lithium Carbonate	4. Prevents release of neurotransmitter
Antipsychotics	5. Blocks receptor

On the following pages are listed many of the psychiatric drugs and their side effects. In our effort to be thorough, we have listed all the possible side effects associated with a particular class of drugs. The more serious or dangerous-sounding side effects are also the most rare. It is, however, important to know the possible risks and be prepared to discuss them with your physician.

I. ANTIPSYCHOTICS. Also known as neuroleptics. The neurotransmitter affected is dopamine.

Trade Name	**Generic Name**
Phenothiazines	
Thorazine	Chlorpromazine
Compazine	Prochlorperazine
Trilafon	Perphenazine
Stelazine	Trifluoperazine

Trade Name	Generic Name
Prolixin HCL	Fluphenazine
Prolixin Decanoate	
Prolixin Ethanoate	
Mellaril	Thiordazine
Serentil	Mesoridazine
Butyrophenone	
Haldol	Haloperidol
Haldol—R	Haloperidol lactate
Thioxanthene	
Navane	Chloprothixane
Dihydroindolone	
Moban	Molindone
Dibenzoexepine	
Loxitane	Loxipine
Clozaril*	Clozepine*

INDICATIONS FOR USE:

1. Psychosis, mania
2. Antiemetic
3. Hiccups
4. Gilles de la Tourette Syndrome
5. Organic Brain Syndrome
6. Acute delerium and drug psychosis

SIDE EFFECTS:

1. Possible weight gain
2. Postural hypotension
3. Urinary retention
4. Skin rashes, sun sensitivity
5. Sedation
6. Liver changes, especially with thorazine
7. ADR—Acute Dystonic Reaction—acute muscle stiff-

ness, neck twisting, eyes moved upward. Reversible, controlled using Cogentin, Artane, Symmetrol

8. TD—Tardive dyskinesias—irreversible movement disorders, e.g, lip smacking, due to overblockage of dopamine transmitter.

9. Parkinson's Syndrome—flat facies, shuffling gait.

10. NMS—Neuroleptic Malignant Syndrome—muscle rigidity, hyperpyrexia, abnormal mental status, tachycardia.

11. Akathisia—subjective sense of restlessness.

12. Mellaril can cause galactorrhea and impotence and possible retinal changes.

13. These medications have a high therapeutic ratio. If a person overdosed with them, a very large amount would have to be consumed.

*Clozaril can cause agranulocytosis, drowziness, sedation, salivation, and possible increase in seizure. It is currently only for treatment resistant schizophrenia. It is still experimental and must be ordered through a drug company where white blood count is closely monitored.

II. ANTIDEPRESSANTS. Neurotransmitters affected are serotonin and norepinephrine.

Trade Name	Generic Name
Tricyclic	
Elavil, Endep	Amitryptiline
Tofranil	Impramine
Aventyl, Pamelor	Nortryptiline
Sinequan, Adepin	Doxepin
Norpramine	Desipramine
Surmontil	Trimipramine
Vivactyl	Protriptyline
Anafranil	Clomipramine
Debenzazepine	

Trade Name	Generic Name
Ascendin	Amoxapine
Tetracyclic	
Ludiomil	Maprotiline
Miscellaneous	
Prozac	Fluoxetine
Zoloft	Sertaline
Desyrel	Tranzodone
Paxil	Paroxetine
MAO Inhibitors	
Parnate	Trancylcypromine
Marplan	Isocarboxid
Nardil	Phelelzine
Aminoketones	
Wellbutrin	Bupropion

INDICATIONS FOR USE:

1. Depression, especially with vegetative signs (insomnia, anorexia, anhedonia).
2. Phobias and agoraphobia with MAO Inhibitors or with Imipramine.
3. MAO Inhibitors for Atypical Depression (somatic symptoms and preoccupations, and anxiety).
4. Clomipramine for Obsessive-Compulsive Disease
5. Bedwetting

These medications are very toxic and have a low therapeutic index. They also have a lag period before they begin to affect the symptoms of depression. With TCAs (antidepressants), a therapeutic blood range must be attained which can be tested through routine blood tests. Prozac and the MAO Inhibitors dosage is titrated according to the relief of symptoms.

SIDE EFFECTS:

1. TCA—Dry mouth, constipation, loss of reading vision, low blood pressure, urinary retention, some EKG

changes, weight gain, sedation. They should not be used with people who have acute angle glaucoma.

2. MAO—Low blood pressure, agitation, impotence, liver toxicity. Since this medication blocks monoamine oxidase, tyramine cannot be metabolized. Any foods containing this amino acid will cause a hypertensive crisis. Foods excluded are anything fermented—especially yogurt, cheese, Chianti wine, processed meats. Patients taking these drugs cannot use over-the-counter cold medications.

3. Prozac will cause agitation, insomnia, diarrhea, and gastric upset the first seven to ten days of treatment; possible headaches and decreased ability in women to reach orgasm. It does not cause weight gain. So far no statistical evidence exists for increased suicidal ideation with Prozac.

4. Wellbutrin can cause seizures.

5. Amoxapine could cause involuntary muscle spasms.

III. ANTIMANIA. It is not clear what the following medicines do to help stabilize moods. All these medications must be followed closely by blood levels. Toxic levels can cause death.

1. Lithium Carbonate takes seven to ten days to be effective.

SIDE EFFECTS:

Nausea (less if capsules are used), weight gain, muscle stiffness, fine hand tremor, asymptomatic hypothyroidism, changes in kidney function including diabetes insipidus, asymptomatic elevation of white blood cell count, skin rashes, thirst.

2. Carbamazepine (tegretol). Originally used for seizure control, tegretol has been found to control bipolar disorder either alone or in combination with lithium.

SIDE EFFECTS:
Blurred vision, dizziness, sedation, and bone marrow suppression.

3. Valproic Acid (depakene) and Devalproex Sodium (depakote) is also an antiseizure medication. It is a third line medication. Blood levels need close monitoring.

SIDE EFFECTS:
Hepatic failure, nausea, vomiting, and sedation.

IV. ANTIANXIETY. The neurotransmitter affected is GABA (Gamma-amino Butyric Acid)

Trade Name	Generic Name
Benzodiazepines	
Librium	Chlordiazepoxide
Valium	Diazepam
Serax	Oxazepam
Tranxene	Chlorozepate
Ativan	Lorazepam
Centrex	Prazepam
Xanax	Alprazolam
Klonopin	Clonazepam
Specialized for Insomnia	
Prosom	Estazolam
Dalmane	Flurazepam
Restoril	Temazepam
Halcion	Triazolam
Non-benzodiazepine	
Visteril	Hydroxyine
Buspar	Buspirone

INDICATIONS FOR USE:
1. Acute anxiety—fastest action is in oral dosages
2. Alcohol and barbiturate withdrawal

3. Muscle relaxant
4. Preoperative anesthesia
5. Anticonvulsants
6. Insomnia
7. Buspar is nonaddictive for control of anxiety. It takes two to three weeks for it to be effective.
8. Use in phobic disorders and panic attacks.

SIDE EFFECTS:
Benzodiazepines cause sedation and physical and/or psychological dependence. Sudden withdrawal of these at high dosages can cause seizures. It is rare for someone using only these drugs to commit suicide. They would need to be taken in conjunction with another medication to cause a fatality.

WHAT IS ELECTRO-CONVULSIVE THERAPY?

Electro-convulsive therapy (or electro-shock therapy or shock therapy) is still used today to treat depression. ECT is used when:

1. A person has not responded to antidepressants or cannot tolerate medication.
2. A person is so depressed he or she has stopped eating. Or, a person is so suicidal that physicians feel they cannot wait three to four weeks for medication to take effect.
3. When elderly or medically ill patients cannot tolerate medication.

ECT induces a seizure which cause the rapid turnover and release of serotonin and epinephrine which reestablishes chemical balance. An ECT course of treatment, averaging six treatments, is administered on one side of the brain. An anesthesiologist is present as well as a psychiatrist. The patient is asleep through the seizure and the body's muscles are totally relaxed.

SIDE EFFECT:
Temporary loss of memory.

GLOSSARY

ABUSE The misuse of a person by another for the selfish purpose of solving problems and meeting needs while totally disregarding the needs and rights of the victim. Abuse can be physical, emotional, or sexual.

ANXIETY Unpleasant and uncomfortable feeling of apprehension and dread of possible danger.

BOND An emotional and intellectual investment two people have in one another that creates a mutual sense of worth and importance.

BOUNDARY The deliberate setting of limits to distinguish one person from another. Boundaries enforce autonomy and separateness, allowing each person to have a sense of self-ownership.

COMFORT To soothe someone in grief, anxiety, or pain.

COMPASSION A deep concern for someone who is suffering.

CONFIDENTIALITY The condition or state of trust one has in another concerning matters of a private nature.

CONFLICT Internal or external discord or opposition of feelings, ideas, or actions.

DEPRESSION Pervasive and sustained feeling of sadness, despair, hopelessness, and worthlessness.

EMPATHY The ability to enter into a person's feelings.

GUILT A feeling of self-reproach from believing that one has done something wrong.

MOOD Predominant feeling or state of mind.

PANIC ATTACK A sudden feeling of terror and impending doom. Symptoms include: chest pains, palpitations, shortness of breath, dizziness, tingling of hands and feet, sweating, nausea, and fear of losing control.

PRIVATE Belonging to some particular person or belonging to one's self.

REPRESSION A defense mechanism where an idea or feeling is excluded from the conscious mind.

SECRET Something made, done, or conducted without the knowledge of others.

SELF Personal identity including one's own interests, welfare, and potential. The essence of being.

SELF-ESTEEM The positive and negative feelings a person associates with his self-image.

SELF-IMAGE The mental picture people have about themselves.

SHAME A personal sense of being flawed or inferior.

SYMPATHY The act of identifying or feeling the same way as another.

TERMINATION A technical psychiatric term for when therapy is finished.

TRADITION The handing down of beliefs, customs, and ideas from one generation to the next by word of mouth or practice.

TRANSFERENCE Displacement of feelings, thoughts, and behaviors, originally experienced in relation to significant childhood figures, onto current relationships.

VULNERABLE Susceptible to being hurt or wounded.

WORKING THROUGH A process of therapy where a person acknowledges the conflicts and feelings behind the problems leading to resolution.

ENDNOTES

Chapter 2

1. James Willwerth, "A Museum of Hate," *Time,* (15 February 1993), 54.
2. John White, *Masks of Melancholy: A Christian Physician Looks at Depression and Suicide* (Downers Grove, Illinois: InterVarsity Press, 1982), 75.
3. Ibid., 51
4. Karl Menninger, *Man Against Himself* (New York: Harcourt, Brace and World, 1938), 13
5. Josh McDowell, *His Image . . . My Image* (San Bernardino, California: Here's Life Publishers, 1984), 96.

Chapter 3

1. David Van Biema, "A Clear View of Heaven," *Life,* (November 1991), 38.
2. Ibid., 31
3. David Seamands, *Putting Away Childish Things* (Wheaton, Illinois: Victor Books, 1982), 9.

Chapter 4

1. William Shakespeare, *Hamlet* (Act 4, Scene 1).
2. Joyce Huggett, *Listening to Others: How One Woman Discovered a Healing Art* (Downers Grove, Illinois: InterVarsity Press, 1988), 90.

Chapter 5

1. Lawrence J. Crabb, Jr. and Dan B. Allender, *Encouragement: The Key to Caring* (Grand Rapids: Zondervan, 1984), 20.
2. Margery Williams, *The Velveteen Rabbit* (New York: Avon Books, 1975), 13.

Chapter 7

1. Joseph Stein, *Fiddler on the Roof* (New York: Crown Publishers, 1964), 2.
2. Ibid., 9.
3. Ibid., 113.
4. Harriet Goldhor Lerner, Ph.D., *The Dance of Intimacy* (New York: Harper and Row, 1989), 10.
5. Stein, *Fiddler,* 68.

Chapter 8

1. Harriet Goldhor Lerner, Ph.D., *The Dance of Intimacy* (New York: Harper and Row, 1989), 35.
2. Ibid.
3. Lawrence J. Crabb, Jr., *The Marriage Builder: A Blueprint for Couples and Counselors* (Grand Rapids: Zondervan, 1982).

Chapter 10

1. William Styron, *Darkness Made Visible—A Memoir of Madness* (New York: Vintage Books, 1992), 69.

Chapter 12

1. Beverly Engel, M.F.C.C., *Partners in Recovery* (Los Angeles: Lowell House, 1991), 40.

Chapter 13

1. From C.S. Lewis, *The World's Last Night,* quoted in *Christianity Today* (11 January 1993), 34.
2. Thomas H. Johnson, Ed., *The Complete Works of Emily Dickinson* (Little Brown & Company, 1960), 116.

Appendix

1. Adapted from William M. Patterson, M.D., "Evaluation of suicidal patients: The SAD PERSONS Scale," *Psychosomatics* (April 1983, Vol. 24, No. 4), 343–49.

2. Definitions taken from:
Diagnostic and Statistical Manual of Mental Disorders (American Psychiatric Association).
What You Should Know about Psychiatric Drugs by Stuart Yodot Sky, M.D., Robert E. Hales, M.D., and Tom Ferguson, M.D. (New York: Grove Weiderfield).
Review of General Psychiatry, (Lange Medical Publishers).
The New Harvard Guide to Psychiatry (Belknap Press of Harvard University).